THE BOARDING S

They were children. Put on a train in a strange land, they waved goodbye to a parent as they headed to an educational institution that, unbeknownst to them, was to become their new home. Separated from their loving families, they strived to meet the expectations of the grownups and, in some cases, to rebel against them. Now, independent women, compassionate mothers and astute professionals, they look back on their youth in the 1960s and 1970s to make sense of why they were sent away, and to give meaning to the sources that have sustained them over the years.

Ex-boarders themselves, Latham and Ferdows provide vivid and emotionally embodied narratives of everyday lives in *The Boarding School Girls*. This remarkable collection of stories explores key issues of identity and lifespan development to seek understanding of the influence of national, religious and family culture on development within two conflicting sets of cultural values. It combines unique qualitative data with illuminating tales of resilience and accomplishment in what is likely to simultaneously inform and inspire readers with feelings of joy and sadness, love and hate, abandonment and hope, but mainly trust and forgiveness.

The stories of eleven 'little rich' Persian girls are a nostalgic reminder of their past cross-cultural ordeals, a pragmatic perspective on psychological implications of boarding school education in Britian, and a celebration of the possibilities of the future. *The Boarding School Girls* is valuable reading for students in cultural, developmental and educational psychology and the humanities, as well as clinical psychologists and educators looking at the impact of boarding school on adolescent development.

Soosan Daghighi Latham is a Professor at York University and an Associate Coach with the Niagara Institute in Toronto. A PhD graduate of the University of Toronto, she is a former Vice President of Human Resources at J.P. Morgan Chase, and Assistant Dean of Executive Programs at Rotman School of Business, University of Toronto.

Roya Movahedi Ferdows is an MBA graduate from Johns Hopkins University with a Post Master's degree from George Washington University. Following several years of working in the corporate world, she is currently an Executive/Leadership Coach, focusing her time on supporting clients to find work/life balance and develop into better leaders.

'One of the greatest gifts we can give our children is the ability to adapt to other cultures, but there is always some risk of alienation from one's own. This interview-based study of Iranian high school girls sent to English boarding schools vividly illustrates these two issues and the diverse ways in which individuals respond to the challenge, and should inform ongoing efforts to bring cross-cultural understanding into education.'

– Mary Catherine Bateson Ph.D., *Cultural Anthropologist*

'As the world struggles to understand how to become a truly global community, we need a much deeper understanding of how people successfully transcend single-culture identities. Latham and Ferdows' fascinating new book, *The Boarding School Girls: Developmental and Cultural Narratives*, offers us profound insights through the lens of young Persian girls who, after being uprooted by revolution, developed as young women and successful adults while immersed in a foreign country and deprived of contact with their family. The stories the authors reveal not only inspire but also guide us in learning to appreciate "the other". Read *The Boarding School Girls*. You won't regret it.'

– Nancy J. Adler, *S. Bronfman Professor of Management, McGill University, Montreal, Author,* Leadership Insight *(Routledge)*

'Migration in search of better futures is now a global pursuit. What can we learn from looking back four decades about being strangers in strange places? *The Boarding School Girls* tells the stories of 11 Persian girls, each of whom found herself in a strange place, an English boarding school. Latham and Ferdows offer deep insight into the experiences and development of those who as children willfully or by necessity searched for better futures and today have become world citizens.'

– Milton D. Hakel, *Ohio Eminent Scholar Emeritus, Bowling Green State University, USA*

THE BOARDING SCHOOL GIRLS

Developmental and Cultural Narratives

Soosan Daghighi Latham
Roya Movahedi Ferdows

Routledge
Taylor & Francis Group
LONDON AND NEW YORK

First published 2018
by Routledge
2 Park Square, Milton Park, Abingdon, Oxon OX14 4RN

and by Routledge
711 Third Avenue, New York, NY 10017

Routledge is an imprint of the Taylor & Francis Group, an informa business

© 2018 Soosan Daghighi Latham and Roya Movahedi Ferdows

The right of Soosan Daghighi Latham and Roya Movahedi Ferdows to be identified as authors of this work has been asserted by them in accordance with sections 77 and 78 of the Copyright, Designs and Patents Act 1988.

All rights reserved. No part of this book may be reprinted or reproduced or utilised in any form or by any electronic, mechanical, or other means, now known or hereafter invented, including photocopying and recording, or in any information storage or retrieval system, without permission in writing from the publishers.

Trademark notice: Product or corporate names may be trademarks or registered trademarks, and are used only for identification and explanation without intent to infringe.

British Library Cataloguing-in-Publication Data
A catalogue record for this book is available from the British Library

Library of Congress Cataloging-in-Publication Data
Names: Latham, Soosan Daghighi, author. | Ferdows, Roya Movahedi, author.
Title: The boarding school girls: developmental and cultural narratives / Soosan Daghighi Latham, Roya Movahedi Ferdows.
Description: Abingdon, Oxon; New York, NY: Routledge, 2018. | Includes bibliographical references and index.
Identifiers: LCCN 2017009325 | ISBN 9781138730656 (hardback: alk. paper) | ISBN 9781138730687 (pbk.: alk. paper) | ISBN 9781315189291 (ebook)
Subjects: LCSH: Girls–Education–Iran–Case studies. | Boarding school students–Iran–Case studies. | Girls–Iran–Social conditions–Case studies.
Classification: LCC LC2372 .L37 2018 | DDC 373.180830955–dc23
LC record available at https://lccn.loc.gov/2017009325

ISBN: 978-1-138-73065-6 (hbk)
ISBN: 978-1-138-73068-7 (pbk)
ISBN: 978-1-315-18929-1 (ebk)

Typeset in Bembo
by Deanta Global Publishing Services, Chennai, India

We dedicate this book to our guardian, Mrs Talieh Peck. Unbeknownst to her, she was instrumental in connecting the two of us and inspiring a bond that resulted in the writing of this book. We are grateful to her for creating a space that allowed us to form new friendships and develop a deeper connection with old friends.

Her story is told separately to honour her memory and to elaborate on the traditional Iranian cultural values as they pertain to the Persian Girls.

CONTENTS

Manifesto of the brave and brokenhearted ix
Preface x

PART I
The shaping of a life 1

   Introduction 3
1 Father knows best 7
2 It was what it was 23
3 This too shall pass 31
   Summary 40

PART II
A life lived 43

   Introduction 45
4 Saghi or Sally? 49
5 Letters of hope 60
6 The rebel within 67
7 Mozart, my friend 76
8 What is the use of crying? 85
   Summary 95

PART III
Lives unknown — 97

    Introduction — 99

  9 Playing nice — 101

10 It could have been — 111

11 Passing it on — 120

    Summary — 125

PART IV
Lives we shared — 127

    Final thoughts — 141

Appendix I: Our Guardian, Mrs Peck — *145*
Appendix II: The writing of this book — *150*
Exhibit I: The Persian girls' profiles — *154*
Exhibit II: Questions for guided conversation — *156*
Exhibit III: Classified interview themes — *158*
Index — *162*

MANIFESTO OF THE BRAVE AND BROKENHEARTED[1]

There is no greater threat to the critics
and the cynics and fear mongers
Than those of us who are willing to fall
Because we have learned how to rise.

With skinned knees and bruised hearts:
We choose owning our stories of struggle,
Over hiding, over hustling, over pretending.

When we deny our stories, they define us.
When we run from struggle, we are never free.
So we turn toward the truth and look it in the eye.

We will not be characters in our stories.
Not villains, not victims, not even heroes.

We are the authors of our lives.
We write our own daring endings.

We craft love from heartbreak,
Compassion from shame,
Grace from disappointment,
Courage from failure.

Showing up is our power.
Story is our way home. Truth is our song.
We are brave and brokenhearted.
We are rising strong.

Note

1 Excerpt from *Rising Strong: The Reckoning, the Rumble, the Revolution*. By Brené Brown, copyright 2015 by Brené Brown. LLC. Used by permission of Spiegel & Grau, an imprint of Random House, a division of Penguin Random House LLC. All rights reserved.

PREFACE

We met for the first time in Tehran in 1978. While living in Iran, our lives progressed along different paths though they occasionally crossed in social settings. When we met in San Francisco in 2012, more than thirty years later, we found ourselves reminiscing about our childhood experiences, our early lives in England and who we had become as adults. The discovery that we had spent our adolescent years in a boarding school, shared the same guardian, lived as next-door neighbours in Bournemouth during our holidays with designated English families, and more importantly, that we both had unresolved questions about our past, inspired the writing of this book.

This chance encounter and the subsequent discussion that day in rainy San Francisco triggered the desire to learn more about our time at boarding school. We were curious about our guardian Mrs Peck. Who was she? What was she like as a woman? We wondered about other women who acted as guardians or mother figures for us. Who were our teachers? What were they like? What kind of influence did they have on us as young girls? We compared our experiences with that of our sisters who also went to boarding school and wondered about the personal experiences of other Iranian women who grew up in British boarding schools. How would they describe their time away from home at such a young age? Why were they sent away at that time? Where were they today? What did they consider to be the impact of their experiences on how they had navigated their lives? Who had they become as adults? The questions seemed endless. They went beyond the subject of boarding school and extended to our lives as girls born in Iran, and our development as adolescent girls.

Looking back to more than thirty years of life in the West, we noted that the specific cross-cultural layer that we had experienced as children in England, added to the complexity of understanding the boarding school phenomenon and our individual experiences. It was in this context that we found ourselves reflecting on the Iranian culture, the impact of the 1979 Islamic Revolution and the disruption it had on our lives. We explored the role of women in a society where misogyny continued to manifest itself in many ways and in particular in the patriarchal practices within families. We were disheartened with the thought that the revolution had systematically entrenched this practice making it even more acceptable to the population, men and women, at large.

The bloody revolution had resulted in the demise of the fifty-year-old Pahlavi Dynasty and the overthrow of the Shah of Iran, Mohammad Reza Shah Pahlavi, who took the throne in 1941 following his father Reza Pahlavi. Often referred to as the 'Last Shah of Iran', he was a secular Muslim monarch sent into exile after the Iranian Revolution of 1979, when Iran became an Islamic Republic. He died in 1980 in exile in Egypt. During the Pahlavi reign, Iran had been supported by the British and later by the U.S. and other Western powers. At that time, we lived in a class of society, though Islamic at its core, that appeared to have embraced Western values and way of life. However, in late 1970s, Ayatollah Ruhollah Khomeini, an Iranian cleric living in exile in France, led an underground movement mobilizing groups of students, leftist intellectuals and Islamic organizations towards civil resistance, strikes and demonstrations within Iran, paralyzing the country economically. Because of his extremist Islamic views, he had been exiled by the Shah's father, Reza Pahlavi. Khomeini's rise to power eventually, on 16 January 1979, resulted in the overthrow of the monarchy, the ousting of the Shah and abdication of his family into exile. Khomeini returned to Iran from France as the Supreme Leader of the new Islamic Republic of Iran in December 1979.

With the Islamic rule in place, life in Iran changed for all. This was true in particular for women who were ordered to abide by the religious code of conduct, cover their hair and their body, and live somewhat socially segregated from the men. It was as a result of the revolution that we, the authors, now find ourselves living in North America. It was also in this context that we concluded that knowledge about young Persian girls' experiences at boarding school had the potential to add not only to the literature on developmental psychology, but also to understanding cross-cultural influences on the development of young adolescents. In addition to contributing to the field of psychology, we believe that the stories of young girls at boarding school are likely to provoke women, with similar experiences as ours, to make sense of their own lives and give meaning to their own journeys. As such, we set out to explore and understand childhood experiences of girls at British boarding schools through the eyes of Persian girls who were placed in a variety of schools during the mid-1960s and 1970s.

Our search for other Persian women who had attended boarding school during this period resulted in a list of thirty women who are now spread across continents. Many were friends we had known all our lives, while others we found through word of mouth. The women whose stories you are about to read either chose to leave Iran because of their disdain toward the new authoritarian regime and its Islamic values, or were forced to leave because of their family's associations with the monarchy and the previous government. We are indebted to these nine women who agreed to share their stories. Their courage and expressions of vulnerability opened up space for us all to collectively explore our youthful experiences in meaningful ways. They opened their hearts in ways that they may not have done in the past and for that we are grateful. Their trust in us to hold their stories, without judgment, speaks to the deeply embedded bond of friendship formed among many of us at a young age. In retelling the stories, we have stayed true to their voices as they were expressed in our interviews. Each interview was unique in how it unfolded, but they all triggered new thoughts as we attempted to understand each life story and at the same time identify common themes. While our boarding school journeys share similarities, the salient character of each woman, the circumstances in which she was sent away and how each of us coped varies, making every story unique. We are immensely thankful to Azy, Dory, Fereshteh, Roxane, Saghi, Sheila, Shirley, Shoreh and Soheila for making the writing of this book possible.

PART I
The shaping of a life

INTRODUCTION

What would you have me do?
Where will you have me go?
What would you have me say, and to whom?

A Course in Miracles[1]

During the 1960s, America was on the verge of the sexual revolution. Betty Friedan's book *The Feminine Mystique*, in which she highlights the need for women to fulfil their dreams outside the home, appeared to have sparked a second wave of the feminist movement. The ripple effects of this movement were only just being felt in Britain, where women continued to depend on their fathers or husbands economically, where traditional early-age marriage was still the norm and where contraceptive pills were only prescribed to married women. By the 1970s, however, the Western world beyond America appeared to have opened up to women somewhat, but in Iran, as Westernized as it was in that era, the rules of social and political engagement for women, particularly young girls, remained the same. At that time, Mohammad Reza Shah's political and social ideology for a great civilization was in full force, symbolized by countrywide festivals of art, music and culture, culminating in the nation's grand celebration of its 2500-year anniversary. The Iranian economy was booming with the increased price of oil and the Shah's 'White Revolution'[2] was in effect. While the Iranian society attempted to transform itself, privately within most families, it continued to be a time of suppressed liberalism and rejection of Western feminism, which was regarded as a capitalist promotion of women as 'sex objects' and 'consumers'. The fundamental family culture, influenced by the rules of Islam as the dominant religion, remained male dominated for all classes of society.

Ironically, the government of Iran deemed education of women essential. Women were expected to participate in the modernization of Iran in their role as the bearer and nurturers of the nation's children as its future citizens.[3] This expectation encouraged the more progressive women to take advantage of the new economic opportunities and enter society as employees, employers and public servants working alongside men. While doing so, however, they remained legally subservient to the will of a father, brother or husband. They needed their father's or husband's consent to marry, to work or to travel. A father maintained responsibility for all the decisions in his daughter's life and, once married, that responsibility fell on her husband's shoulders alone. Meanwhile, the primary goal of women's education continued to be preparing them for the traditional roles of a dutiful wife and a devoted mother. This was in stark contrast to the family expectations from a boy and the role he played as a father, brother or a husband.

Among Iranian families, considerable value was placed on the birth of a boy and most parents, regardless of their status in society, expected to have at least one son to carry on their good name. The Shah himself was forced to divorce his beloved Fawzia because she was unable to bear him a male heir to the throne. Fawzia was an Egyptian princess who married the Shah to strengthen the political alliance between Iran and Egypt. Their only daughter, Shahnaz, was not recognized as heir and had no political role in Iran. The Shah later also divorced his second wife, Soraya, the daughter of an Iranian nobleman and a diplomat, because she could not bear any children. Soraya's mother was of German origin and she had grown up in Berlin. She returned to Europe after her divorce. In 1959, in order to produce an heir, the Shah married his third wife, Queen Farah, born to upper-class parents of Persian descent. Farah's father was an officer in the Imperial Armed Forces. She bore four children, with her first-born, Reza, becoming Crown Prince and heir to the throne. Divorcing a wife and remarrying in order to bear a son was not unusual among Iranian families.

The Iranian legal system and cultural values, as well as the societal class, defined the general code of conduct with a clear double standard based on gender. From the start, boys were placed higher on the totem pole and treated with a different set of rules than girls. As they grew into men, the expectation was that as the sole breadwinner, they provide the financial and social governance of their family. A son ranked second to the patriarch and, when mature enough, demanded similar dutiful behaviour from the rest of the household and in particular the women. The law supported this male dominance prevalent in the majority of households by considering one man's vote equivalent to that of two women. It also attributed a higher percentage of inheritance to the son as opposed to the wife or a daughter, thus ensuring financial superiority and power. Once married, the man, now a husband and a father, was the king of the household, respected and often feared by family members, especially young daughters who learned early to obey the rules and do as they were told. In cases of divorce, young girls became their father's responsibility after the age of seven (age two for boys) and were governed according to the father's rules and regulations.

When it came to the upbringing of girls, among the Iranian upper class in particular, there was a bias toward family name and reputation. Other people's perceptions of the family and their daughter's behaviour mattered. Within this class, people knew (or knew of) each other and took account of their actions. This closed circle created an added pressure for the family to ensure that their reputation was not scarred in any way by the behaviour of their daughters. This was particularly true in the capital city of Tehran, where young girls who were seen out and about the town were considered 'free' or 'loose'. In stricter families, dating or being seen around boys, other than those who were members of the extended family or circle of friends, was frowned upon. Sexual interactions amongst girls and boys was disapproved of – a girl's virginity was linked directly to the reputation of the family. Although education of girls was important, finding a career was an exception as the ultimate goal for a daughter was to attract a good husband. A 'good' husband was considered to be a man who had a respectable profession, preferably a doctor or an engineer, was financially stable and came from a reputable family. For these families, among the many reasons their daughters were sent abroad to boarding school was that they could grow up in a controlled environment while receiving the best education, so as to come back as a *khanom*, a lady.

Royalty or not, a boy or a girl, Iranian children's upbringing was in general influenced by a combination of maternal love and strong discipline by the father. The spirit in which they were brought up was in deep contrast to the growing belief in the West that 'children don't belong to us – they are little strangers who arrive in our lives and give us the pleasure and duty of caring for them – but we don't own them. We help them become who they are'.[4] The typical pressures and expectations that Iranian parents had of their children, and in particular their daughters, discouraged any form of independence, self-expression or even inclusion in the decisions that would shape their lives. The father alone made the decisions, no discussion. Children were to be seen, occasionally, and not heard.

We, the storytellers, were brought up with strong, upper-class family values. We enjoyed a privileged life with respect to education and financial status, living a fairy-tale Western lifestyle. Yet, when it came to the decisions about our lives, such as sending us abroad for education, we generally had little or no knowledge, involvement or understanding of what was about to happen. To us, the idea of getting on a plane to go to a school in a foreign land seemed exciting, an adventure worth looking forward to, but we had no real perception of the impending separation and distance, nor an understanding of what that change could mean. Our lives were crafted first by our parents' critical decisions to send us thousands of miles away and, later, by our English educators and caregivers. Very little was expected from us other than obedience and compliance, first to our parents' expectations and later to the expectations of authority figures in our schools. At the time of our departure, we all complied and accepted our fate without question. In our stories, we seek the chance to ask those questions even as we have already lived the answers, each in our own way.

Notes

1 From Lesson 71, *A Course in Miracles*, www.acim.org/Lessons/lesson.html?lesson=71 Retrieved 16 February 2017.
2 The White Revolution was a series of land reforms representing the Shah's attempt to gain popularity among the rural population, symbolized as a step toward Westernization.
3 In her book, *Women and the Political Process in Twentieth-Century Iran* ((1995), University Press, Cambridge, U.K., p. 112), Parvin Paidar describes extensively the role of women in shaping the political agenda.
4 Steinem, G. (1992), *Revolution from Within*, Little Brown & Company, Toronto, Canada, p. 65.

1
FATHER KNOWS BEST

Roya's story
Charters Towers School, Bexhill-on-Sea, Sussex (1964–1970)

I was six when my parents moved us to the U.S. My father, an obstetrician/gynecologist, had secured a fellowship at Johns Hopkins Hospital for a two-and-a-half-year engagement. My mother, a midwife, was also going to study cytotechnology at the same hospital with the dream of becoming a pioneer in the new field of cytology (the study of cells), a field still unknown in Iran. My father left for the U.S. before us and found a summer camp, Camp Odeta in Connecticut, where he would be the resident physician, and my sister Vida and I could be registered as campers for free. At the camp, we were totally immersed in the English language in preparation for our school and the work ahead, which was to begin in the autumn.

This was the first time I experienced the hollow feeling of being pulled away from my parent's loving, nurturing arms. We were to participate in the camp programs with the other campers with little contact with my parents. I was a very shy and attached child, always needing and longing for the closeness and touch of my parents. I replaced the emptiness I felt by staying close to the counsellors, and remember them as beautiful, young and friendly women. My predominant memories from that camp are of sadness. On occasion, especially at mealtimes, I would get a glimpse of my parents and was able to grab a hug or touch from them. But most of the time I felt the soon-to-be-familiar pangs of separation.

Thankfully, camp did not last long. A month later, we piled into our car and drove to Baltimore to start a new chapter of our lives. It was the end of August. We lived on the top floor of a house and the owner, a kind, grandmotherly lady, lived on the ground floor. For two and a half years we went to school, learned English, and followed the American way of life. My parents had a very productive and worthwhile time at Johns Hopkins that catapulted both of their careers to a higher level of excellence. We were hesitant to leave the U.S. at the end of our sojourn, yet excited to rejoin our friends and family back home.

I was eight on our return to Tehran. Having started school in the U.S. and with only English literacy, Vida and I were placed in the Community School in Tehran. Located in the city centre, the large building was in the middle of a big, tree-filled garden, which housed all the classrooms. School was fun and it felt like an American island in the heart of Tehran. Unlike most of the other students who had private, chauffeur-driven cars, our transport to the school was Rasouli, our helper/servant who had lived in our house for years. He was a big man, and probably only in his forties although he had lost most of his teeth and appeared very old to our young eyes. We trusted him and felt very protected by him. He loved us like his own and we loved him, though we had fun teasing him from time to time. In the mornings, he would hail a taxi outside our home to accompany us to school, drop us off at the school gate and pick us up at the end of the school day.

In those days, there were not many occasions for parents to come to school. Sometimes my mother would come for a teacher/parent conference but on one rare occasion, for no particular reason other than perhaps family logistics, my father came to school to pick us up. That was the day Vida's and my life changed. This was probably the first time my father had visited our school! Let it be said that my father was very conservative and strict and even the years in the U.S. had not liberalized him! When he came looking for us, he witnessed a very liberal 'Americanized' atmosphere: girls and boys holding hands, hugging and kissing in different corners of the school. This surprised and shocked him. At that moment, he decided that his girls were not in the right place and that he would have to find an alternative for their education. This was three years after our return from the U.S.

My father had heard of other families in Tehran who were sending their children to England. Together with my mother, they decided this would be the course for our future education. Although my parents were neither rich nor elite, they always wanted the best for us, disregarding the hardships they would face. Both were dedicated to their work and had a very active social life. They did not have time to focus on our studies. So, they presented this idea to Vida, who, being adventurous, considered it to be an exciting opportunity to explore without the strict scrutiny of parents. How mistaken she was!

At the time, my father was part owner of Jame Hospital in Tehran. The administrator of this hospital was a retired general who had sent his two daughters, Mahvash and Farideh, to Charters Towers School, in Bexhill-on-Sea, Sussex. The eldest daughter had graduated and was now back in Iran and married. She also happened to be one of my father's patients. Her younger sister had begun her studies at the school the previous year. After talking to Mahvash and getting her feedback as a student, my father, together with another colleague, decided that Vida, thirteen, and Mitra, twelve, the colleague's daughter, would leave together.

Now, the one thing left to do was to find a guardian who would take on responsibility for Vida in England. My father's mentor, Dr S—, for whom he had great respect and whose advice he trusted, suggested his sister Mrs Peck, who lived in England. My father had already met her on one of her visits to Iran and knew he could entrust his daughter to her capable hands.

The day arrived for my sister's grand departure.

> Vida was excited to go on this new adventure and have the opportunity for liberty and independence. I was sad to see my sister leave me. In those years, air travel abroad was considered a luxury. In fact, going to the airport was a family outing. People went early to have time to visit the restaurant, to watch the airplanes as they landed and the passengers as they walked off the plane, or to watch the travellers wave goodbye to their loved ones as they climbed up into what seemed like an enormous vessel! That day, several of my aunts, uncles and cousins had come to bid farewell to my sister, bearing gifts of Persian delights to take with her as souvenirs on her trip. I remember my sadness as I held Vida and kissed her goodbye. I didn't want to see her go. I still had my brother, who was nine years younger, at home with me, but he could not fill the void. She, on the other hand, was excited and, with her new friend, was off to her adventure in the new land.

The year was 1963. The most common form of international communication was through airmail letters and perhaps the annual birthday telegram. The postal service was slow from Iran, taking weeks for a letter to travel across the continent. International telephone calls were not only extremely expensive they were only permitted in emergencies at the schools. There were no cell phones, Skype, email or Facetime!

In hindsight, the thought of sending a child off in an airplane and not knowing when or how they arrived is inconceivable for most mothers today. But we were living in a world then that was much safer. Crime was not what it is today. Nonetheless, I can't imagine anyone taking that kind of risk with twelve or thirteen-year-old kids. I believe that once Vida arrived, Mrs Peck sent a telegram confirming her arrival.

> I was lonely without my big sister. We were very close and had done everything together. During our year apart, Vida wrote letters recounting her wonderful experiences and adventures, encouraging me to join her the following year. As it came closer to the summer months, she continued promoting the experiences we would have together in England.

I only learned the truth about her difficult and trying days when I too was experiencing them. I believe that since she had agreed to go, she didn't want to worry our parents. I later found out that Vida's experience at school was not at all what she had portrayed and that there was abuse and some painful times. She had not divulged this perhaps for fear that I would not follow her. She may have thought that as long as we were together, our time there would be better. Although my parents never pressured me to go, their plan was to send one daughter and then the second, and eventually our baby brother, when he was old enough.

> I was sceptical. I knew I needed to be around my parents and loved the connection I had with them, especially my mother, to whom I felt extremely close. The thought of not being held and kissed by her every day was painful. But, although there was always help in the house, my parents were rarely around, and with Vida's departure I felt lonely. She was my big sister and extremely influential in my life. I looked up to her. So, the idea of being with my big sister again was becoming more and more attractive.

In those years, parents were not immediately involved with their children. Young professionals, such as my parents, were socially active, going to parties many nights. This meant a lot of upkeep for the women. Good, ready-made clothing was not easily available so women spent considerable time purchasing fabric, picking a fashionable style and having it tailor-made. In addition, there was at least a weekly visit to the hairdresser and manicurist. And if the party was in your house, there was a week of preparation. In addition to all this, my mother had started a Cytology School at Tehran University with her professors at Johns Hopkins and had an extremely busy professional life. My father, too, spent long hours on his private practice as well as being a professor at the University of Tehran. My parents' busy schedules did not allow much time with the children. I didn't realize it then, but we hardly saw them during the week. Perhaps that is why I had such an attachment to them. I never felt I had enough of their presence in my life.

> With the arrival of summer, Vida came home. I was excited to have my big sister back with me. Her suitcase filled with new clothes and her stories riveted me. She was thrilled to be taking me back with her, and told me all about the good times we would have. I had just celebrated my twelfth birthday when it was time to pack for my new life in England.

A letter was sent to Mrs Peck with the necessary information to pick us up at the airport. As it started to become a reality, those last few weeks became emotionally difficult for me.

> I remember that familiar heaviness in my heart as I prepared to leave my parents and little brother, whom I loved dearly. Once again, aunts, uncles, cousins and grandparents came bearing gifts to see the two young sisters off on our journey. Like two grown-ups, hand-in-hand, Vida and I hugged, kissed and shed a few tears as we said goodbye to our family. I still remember the pain of pulling myself from the warm embrace of my beautiful mother and strong, loving father. But I was not going to let them see me cry. That would hurt them too much, I thought. I still fill up with tears as I recall those excruciating goodbyes fifty years ago!
>
> The airline hostess led us inside the airplane. As soon as I was on board, I broke down and cried for many hours, as Vida tried to console me while holding herself together, comforting me as best she could. She had instantly taken on the responsibility of being her younger sister's keeper in a strange land.
>
> As a parent, myself, I can imagine the torment my parents may have felt to send their two young daughters to an unknown land, handing over their responsibility to a virtual stranger. It would be at least a few days before they would hear of our safe arrival. The anticipation of the telegram must have been agonizing! I still can't comprehend the enormity and consequential emotions they possibly experienced because of their decision!
>
> Finally, we arrived at Heathrow. There was Mrs Peck, meticulously dressed in her hat and gloves, waiting to receive her old and new wards. Just to see her face, a mature lady, warm and welcoming, was comforting to me. Mrs Peck was in control from here. She called the porter, got our luggage and called a cab. Excitement was beginning to take the place of anxiety and despair. The cab ride was the beginning of my adventure. We arrived at night, to damp rainy weather, as is expected in London, but the yellow streetlights reflecting against the wet asphalt fascinated me.
>
> To this day, I love British cabs: the square boxes, roomy and protected, with the seats facing each other. The slow rocking of the vehicle adds to its

infinite charm. Every time I return to London the memories of the cab rides to the airport bring a wave of nostalgia and dance vividly in my memories.

Mrs Peck lived in Kew Gardens, a beautiful area just outside London. We arrived at her large, spacious house (or so it seemed at the time!), with exquisitely styled furniture, and a courtyard filled with vegetation and flowers. She showed us to our room and then offered us supper (in England supper is a warm drink with cheese and crackers or biscuits later in the evening). We were to sleep soon after our arrival because the next day we had a heavily laden schedule of errands in preparation for school.

We woke up early, got ready and were off, uniform list in hand, to purchase all the requirements from Dickins & Jones, the assigned department store for Charters Towers School uniform. Everything had to be in accordance with the school list. There were the weekday and Sunday uniforms, including a coat, felt hat (for the winter) and boater hat (for the summer), sports uniform, and so on. We would change into our 'home clothes' for tea, but there was also a dress code. Skirt and sweater twin sets for the week, dresses for the weekend. Towels, linen and eiderdown blanket, and all other amenities were purchased in addition to a trunk, to pack all of this and send to the school.

My new wardrobe, now complete, was placed in my black trunk with the gold locks! The Sunday uniform I was to travel in and the weekday uniform, which I needed immediately on arrival at school, were packed in my suitcase. I was very excited about these crisp new clothes and couldn't wait to wear them. The store was to send the trunk separately to arrive soon after. In the years that followed, I would develop a personal attachment to my trunk! It followed me around carrying all my belongings, perhaps as the only constant during those years of impermanence.

The next day the school train was to leave from Victoria station. Vida and I were dressed in our Sunday uniforms – brown pinafore dress, yellow gingham shirt, brown overcoat, brown felt hat, brown leather gloves, brown knee-high socks and brown Mary Jane shoes. Very proper. Accompanied by Mrs Peck, we climbed into the taxi, luggage in tow, and headed for the station. I recall the mixed feeling of anxiety and excitement for the first day in my new school and life, as I would know it from then on.

We arrived to the hustle and bustle of Victoria station. It wasn't difficult to identify the excited group of Charters Towers girls, all uniformly dressed in their brown and gold. There they were, all these twelve to eighteen-year-olds, lugging their big heavy suitcases (without wheels)! I shudder at the memory. Luckily, Mrs Peck, who was with us on this occasion, called a porter to assist. At the train, the mistress in charge checked our names from her list as we bid goodbye to Mrs Peck and boarded the train.

After the initial excitement of witnessing the reunion of the older students started to taper off, the anxiety of being without an older responsible person began to set in and sadness overcame me. Although my acquaintance with

Mrs Peck had only been but a day, she was the only responsible adult in my life in this strange country. Not having her support anymore, I felt the new but now familiar heaviness in my chest, and homesickness for my parents and their loving care and support. However, I was not the only girl crying by now. Many of the first-year girls shared my emotional state, overwhelmed by these unfamiliar surroundings. Fortunately, Vida was not far away, and reached out to comfort and console me. She was excited about seeing her now 'old' friends, and tried to instil that excitement in me.

Finally, we arrived at Bexhill-on-Sea station, where we were loaded onto the school bus. The school looked enormous. It was comprised of four large houses (a fifth house was added in later years), with a large driveway connecting them, and a hedge separating the driveway from the street. The new class of First Formers were all in House One, which was where the bus dropped us off. (My sister, now in House Two, had already been separated from me when we had boarded the bus at the station.)

Miss Sharpus, the school nurse, who was also the matron in charge of House One, greeted us at the door. She was a tall, slender lady, wearing her customary crisp white nurse's uniform, navy waistband and navy cloak, with her soft brown curls held up with pins under her nurse's cap. She always wore her signature bright red lipstick. She had a soft voice, with a friendly, warm, welcoming face. I liked Miss Sharpus from that first moment. She was the kindest matron I had in all the years at school. Although she was a disciplinarian, I was never afraid of her. She was a kind yet strict 'mother' to us. Unlike the other matrons, once we left House One, we remained in contact with Miss Sharpus as the school nurse. It was comforting to know she was the one caring for us when we were sick.

I was sent up to the top floor to find my dorm. It was the only two-bedroom dorm in the House, right under the roof. The ceiling was slanted and I had to take care not to hit my head. My roommate had not yet arrived. I was relieved not to have to share my room with too many other people like in the other dorms, at least for now. My roommate finally arrived; she was a blond blue-eyed British girl who, like me, had an older sister at the school. I later discovered that although she was one of the smartest girls in the class and good at all sports, she was painfully shy, even more than I was, and hence not very sociable. Right to our last year at school, she did not have many friends. I always thought she would become a famous doctor and found out later that she had become a nurse.

Our days began at 7 a.m. with the first bell alerting those who were assigned morning baths that it was time to wake up. After fifteen minutes, the second bell prompted everyone else to get up, wash up and strip the beds (i.e. fold them completely and place them on the chair beside the bed). Then, into our uniforms and down to the dining room for breakfast. It may seem like such a waste of time to strip the beds before breakfast and then make them up again. There was a reason for this. The process of stripping the bed ensured that the sheets were aired each day.

Each week the bottom sheets and pillowcases were washed whereas the top sheet was moved to the bottom and hence washed every other week.

At mealtime, the entire school, including teachers, staff and the headmistress, gathered to eat together. At the front of the dining room a long table was set on a platform for the teachers and staff. The students were assigned tables according to their forms (grade), eight per table with a mistress (teacher) or matron seated at the head. Each week the table assignments and dining hall duties changed. The students were also assigned responsibility for clearing and serving the head table.

Although table manners were important, meal times were fun since we relaxed and enjoyed the meals. After grace, and once everyone at the table was served, we began to eat. The mistress at the head of the table was in charge of serving food and also in charge of our table manners, ensuring we sat up, no elbows on the table, and that we used the cutlery properly. Meals were hearty, delicious and plentiful. My love of British food began here. Breakfasts were elaborate, alternating between poached fish, kippers (I even grew to like fish in the morning!), fried eggs, bacon, sausage, tomatoes, scrambled eggs, fried bread, and plenty of white and brown bread with butter, an assortment of jams, Marmite, honey and tea or milk. We would conjure up games amongst ourselves like 'who could eat the most amount of bread and Marmite in one sitting!'

Assembly started the day's activities.

> The first assembly I attended was also my first encounter with Miss McGarry, the headmistress. She, along with the other teachers, dressed in their black gowns, would walk up to the platform to take their seats after we had all entered the assembly hall – very formal and serious – as we all stood up for their arrival. Classical music would be played on the gramophone, until Miss McGarry permitted us to sit, as she began her address to the students. We would have prayers and sing hymns and then were dismissed to attend our classes.

Every day for high tea, we changed into our home clothes: regulation pleated skirts and sweater twin sets during the week, and dresses on the weekend. Naturally, and to the greatest extent possible, we experimented with hiking the skirts as high as acceptable, if only to experience our own sense of personal style.

After tea, there was time for prep (homework) in our classrooms, with a mistress in charge to ensure there was no talking or sharing of information. Then, back to the common room to read or socialize until bedtime. Each house had its own common room according to the age of the girls. There, we were allowed to play music on our transistor radios, and read our own books, talk or play board games. One night a week we were allowed to watch 'Top of the Pops' and swoon over our favourite singers or groups: The Beatles, Rolling Stones, Tom Jones, Cliff Richards!

Since bedtime was quite early, most girls had flashlights and would read under the covers after lights out. Also, some of the more adventurous girls, who were already aware of their sexuality, would hop into each other's beds and experiment with kissing and exploring each other's bodies. On occasions, they were caught by the matron and reported to Miss McGarry.

We were each assigned a bath or shower, alternating weekly, day or night. Many of the British girls preferred baths, but most of the foreign girls weren't used to them, especially since there was only a few inches of water allowed in the tub. So, we switched when we could to take a shower instead. Some would occasionally bathe together in that little amount of water and sometimes discover or play with each other's bodies. It is reasonable to say that we were exposed to homosexuality at a very early age, at a time when it was not talked about openly. While the girls didn't identify themselves as lesbian, there appeared to be an implicit understanding and acceptance of homosexual behaviour, albeit it wasn't referred to as such.

On the weekends, we carried out errands such as laundry and shoe shining. The matron would inspect our drawers, dorm by dorm, before we were allowed to enjoy free time. Once a month, each House was permitted to walk into town in groups, although we were banned from going into restaurants and Woolworths. Occasionally we sneaked into the local Wimpy (the McDonald's of the time) and bought a hamburger, although it was not easy to go against the rules. Bexhill-on-Sea was a small town inhabited by retirees, many of who acted as spies for the school. They regularly reported student misconduct to Miss McGarry and, somehow, she would discover the culprit!

Saturday nights we had dancing in the auditorium. We dressed in our home clothes, did our hair and looked our best for the occasion. It was not obligatory, but it was our chance to let loose, relax, express our individuality (as much as possible) and play the music of The Kinks, The Beatles, and The Rolling Stones and dance like crazy! Also, it was a chance for the older girls to show off to the younger girls. There was a culture of younger girls having a crush on the older ones; sometimes as a sexual attraction and other times, as a role model. In later years, a Saudi girl had a crush on me. I was three years older than her. The girls with the crush would buy small gifts for their crushes with their pocket money, and secretly slip it to them so that others would not tease them. On Saturday nights, if they were brave enough they would come and ask their crushes to dance. Unlike some other schools, we never had any contact with the local boys' schools; other girls were our only dancing partners!

We loved Sundays. It was different from every other day of the week! After breakfast, the Christian girls dressed in their formal coats and hats, lined up House-by-House to walk to the church. The non-Christians did not go to church, but each religious group and country had their own meeting. Since I was born a Muslim, I went to the Iranian/Muslim group meeting. The oldest girl in each group was in charge of these meetings, during which time we talked and reminisced about our family and friends back home. Apart from these occasions, there was no real communication across the age groups, but this hour on Sundays was different. We were all on a level playing field and connected as compatriots. It was also the only time we were allowed to talk in our native language. At the end of the hour we were required to say a prayer in our religion. The girl in charge would say a *namaz*[1] and we would repeat after her, not knowing what it meant since it was in Arabic. This was when I first questioned religion. Why were we saying a prayer we didn't even understand?

After prayers, we went for the required Sunday walk and fresh air around the school block. I looked forward to the few hours I would have with other Iranian girls to talk in our language, reminisce about our homes, or make plans for the next upcoming holidays.

Sunday lunch was special. It was always exciting to see what was on the menu. Roast beef with gravy, Yorkshire pudding, roast potatoes, peas and treacle tart with custard, or roast chicken, mashed potatoes, green beans and ice cream. It was all so delicious and second helpings were the norm! We ate so much I'm surprised we all didn't turn out overweight! Occasionally, we had a movie on Sunday night in the auditorium, but generally it was a quiet, low-key day. During our free time, when the weather was nice, we laid in the sun, played our transistor radios, read or sunbathed.

> There was a certain air of melancholy in the school on Sundays. Many of the girls went on *exeats*[2] with their families. For us foreign girls, that was exceptional unless, on rare occasions, one of the other girls invited us out. We witnessed the excitement of the other girls throughout the week, and would run to the bedroom window to watch as they met their families, hugged them and were whisked off in their car to an outing, while we visualized their day, outside the confines of the school.

Sometimes the girls who had *exeat* came back with new clothes or tuck (candy), which they occasionally shared with us. There was a feeling of being special if you were one of the lucky ones to get to go on an *exeat*. In the meantime, those of us who were left behind distracted ourselves by writing letters to our families (which we had to do on Sundays anyway), reading and talking.

> My first *exeat* was with my friend Diana. She and I became close friends during the first year at school. I was fascinated by her strikingly blonde/white hair and her beautiful blue eyes. I knew her mother was sick with cancer and that she lived in a town nearby. It was early in the first year of school when one day she was called to Miss McGarry's office and was told her mother had died and that she was to go home for the funeral. This touched me deeply and that day has stayed vividly in my memory. I was very sad for her and couldn't imagine losing my mother. Shortly after, she returned to school and her sadness was palpable. On her next *exeat*, she invited me to go with her.
>
> I don't know what I was expecting, going to a home where such a tragedy had just been experienced, but I know that my exposure to this day impacted me. Needless to say, the mood in their home was very sombre. They lived in a small but modern house on a farm. I could sense immense sadness in her

father. Diana had a younger brother and a baby sister. Her father appeared overwhelmed with the responsibilities left to him after the death of his wife. I felt such compassion and empathy for this man. He cooked us a lunch of poached fish and boiled potatoes. He was making an effort for normalcy during this time of tragedy and devastation, for the sake of his young family. But I was very much looking forward to returning to the safe haven and atmosphere of my school.

The next *exeat* I was invited to go on was with my friend, Shirley (Chapter 6). Shirley and I arrived at the school the same year and I had met her soon after my arrival. As we were both Persian, we immediately became close friends and remain so to this day. On this *exeat*, she had also invited Azy (Chapter 3) and Roxane (Chapter 8), two other Iranian girls who had joined Shirley and me in our form the following year. Together, the four of us became inseparable friends during our time at school.

Shirley's sister arrived in her Jaguar with the maid, who had brought us a beautiful picnic of *baghala polo* (rice with lima beans and dill), my favourite Persian dish to this day. (I wonder if it has remained my favourite because of the memories of that day.) I don't recall where we went to have our picnic, but I believe it was at a park. The lunch was spread out as we savoured the familiar food and enjoyed our outing. After lunch, we went to Hastings to the Grand Hotel for high tea. It was truly a lovely day with my best friends.

> The first time my mother came to visit the school, I recall my excitement the weeks leading up to her arrival. My mother was a beautiful, elegant woman. I was excited to show her off to my friends. She had a visit with Miss McGarry, and we took her around for a tour of the school. We then walked into town and had high tea at the local restaurant. All the while, I was dreading having to let go of her comforting hand for fear that she would disappear from my life again. When I didn't see my family, I managed, but once I did, the separation was excruciatingly painful. Luckily, the holidays were coming up and I had that to look forward to – spending a month with my mother.

In my later years, Shirley MacLaine's daughter became a student at our school. She looked just like her mother. One day there was a rumour that Shirley MacLaine was to visit her daughter at school. All morning we were ready to catch a glimpse of this famous celebrity. Eventually, she arrived in her stretch limousine with her long trailing mink coat, matching mink hat and red bob-styled hair. I was mesmerized standing in the corner of the hallway watching her walk to Miss McGarry's office. She never looked my way, yet it was exciting to be in her presence. I was completely star struck!

At the end of each term, we were allowed a midnight feast. When it was our turn to have a town outing, we shopped for this special event. Occasionally, we would have unauthorized midnight feasts, which were always more fun. I guess we found doing anything outside the regulations of the school more fun! We bought all sorts of food, chips, salami, baguettes, pickles and pickled onions. We would sneak the food into our room and after 'lights out' we would find a corner of the dorm or go into a bathroom and have our little feast. Looking back, I'm sure the matrons knew but turned their heads and ignored these escapades. The noise and nervous giggles must have surely given us away. Occasionally, we were too loud and ended up getting caught and punished. Our usual punishment was that we were banned from changing into our home clothes after school, or, worse, not allowed to go on town outings. This way everyone in the school knew that we were being punished.

Classes were boring. Many of the teachers were widowers from World War II. My favourite teacher was Mr Foster, who taught physics and chemistry. He was an older man (although now that I think of it probably only in his thirties!) He was short but solidly built and carried an excellent posture. He wore round, wire-rimmed glasses and had a head of tight curly black hair. Mr Foster was even-tempered and soft-spoken, but demanded respect. I loved this man; maybe because he was one of the only male figures in this all girls' school, infested with widows and spinsters as teachers. He was married and had two young children. He was an excellent teacher who inspired my interest in science. He was also a sportsman and the hockey and field sports coach.

Another teacher was Mrs Butterfield, who may have been of German origin. She was a cute, stocky, short woman, teaching geography. Although she was odd, she was kind and had a certain warmth and maternal aura about her. She had the habit of enunciating words and stretching them when she talked: 'There are two Americaaas, Souuuuth Americaaa and Norrrth Americaaa', with a quick twitch of her head after each sentence. She amused us.

Miss Elliott, the English teacher, had a habit of opening all her cardigan buttons down to her waist and then closing them up again, as she was teaching Shakespeare! My gym teacher, Mrs Wray, was tall and slim and had a great body. I thought she was very attractive. (Many of the girls had the famous 'crush' on her!) She was kind and friendly. We never heard a harsh word out of her. As I reflect, the kind teachers taught the subjects that I enjoyed and followed in later years. I have become aware of how these formative years can affect a child's mind, creativity and curiosity. This is when children are encouraged or discouraged to follow their dreams.

> I loved to play the piano. I fell in love with it as a child. My fascination was triggered originally by my older cousin Mitra, who had studied piano in Paris. Whenever I was at my aunt's house I would beg her to play. I would just stand next to the piano and be mesmerized by the music and the way she got lost in it. I begged my parents to let me take piano lessons while in Iran, but they said we couldn't afford a piano, plus we didn't have room for one in our house. At school, I would listen to my friend Roxane when she practiced. She was an excellent pianist. Once I found that piano lessons were offered at school, I fulfilled my long-time dream by signing up for lessons.

But I was assigned to a terrible piano teacher. She was creepy. She was a small woman who would sit close to me and every time I made a mistake she would take my small hand into both hers and talk to me, breathing bad breath into my face. I longed to change teachers but wasn't allowed. Needless to say, the days of my piano playing were numbered and seeing as I made little improvement, I quit shortly after. I was satisfied to listen to Roxane practice and live vicariously through her joy and talent for music.

Not all the teachers were nice. Some were harsher and demanding but I believe the culture of the school did not allow too much harshness. Miss McGarry took care of all that! We were all afraid of her. Everyone was – even the teachers, including her mother, Madam. Sometimes Miss McGarry would appear unexpectedly in the classroom and everyone would hustle to be on her best behaviour. If you ever got a smile out of her it was a miracle. How does one instil that kind of fear into people? Many of those interviewed from Charters Towers believe that she should never have been a headmistress. I, on the other hand, believe that for her to keep the kind of order she demanded at that school, she needed to be strict and severe in her position, although perhaps not to the extent she was.

Holidays were long, giving the girls the chance to go home. Christmas and Easter were one month each and summer two and a half months. For my sister and me, Christmas was usually spent in a holiday home; at Easter, my mother would come, and in the summer, we would go back home to Iran. The first few years we stayed with the Hall family for Christmas – a holiday home Mrs Peck had chosen for us in Bournemouth, Hampshire. They were a kind family. Another Iranian girl, a few years older than my sister, was also there with us. She was our guide and friend. I recall Mrs Hall waking us up with a cup of tea in our room in the mornings. The night before Christmas was celebrated with tea and cookies. Our Christmas meal started with eggnog and a wonderful meal of turkey, roast potatoes, Yorkshire pudding, peas, gravy, and for dessert mince pie and Christmas pudding with custard. To this day I continue the tradition of this Christmas menu with my own family. On Boxing Day, the Halls would invite over friends and we would socialize with them. We were immersed and included in the British traditions of celebrating Christmas.

After a couple of years at the Halls', my parents decided that we should spend the holidays in Switzerland to improve our French. We were excited to be going to another country and prepared ourselves for the colder winter. The first year we stayed with an aristocratic Swiss family in Geneva. I think we were given the maid's room because it was actually outside their apartment. Another older Persian girl was with us there. Geneva was fun. It was good to be in a big city where we spent our days walking around the city and shopping. Their sit-down Christmas dinner was more elaborate, but more 'stuffy' and not as homey as the Halls. I wonder why this aristocratic and seemingly rich family would take three boarders over the Christmas holidays?

The following year we were sent to a home in a small ski village in the mountains of Switzerland. The home also served as a day care for small children. This home in a farm town was very different from our first experience. There was an older German girl there as well. She was the assistant for the day care. She became our friend. In the evenings, we would go to the local farm to pick up fresh milk and then to the local bar to have a *pastis* (a local French liquorice alcoholic drink) and cigarettes! At night, we played cards and ate chocolates. I had always loved the idea of skiing, and since we were in this ski village it just seemed so natural to do so, but my strict father did not permit that, believing it to be a dangerous sport. Later, when I ended up going to Switzerland for college, I started skiing without his permission!

> The best holidays were when my mother would visit. One time we stayed at the Cumberland Hotel on Marble Arch. It was quite an expensive hotel at the time, and a luxury to be living there for nearly a month. Other years my mother would rent a small apartment in the Marble Arch area since Oxford Street was one of the best areas to shop, and that was her second objective in being in England! It was fun to have our small apartment and have my mother cook our favourite Persian meals, spend time talking, laughing and shopping together. At the start of the holidays, my mother would give my sister and me some money (I believe it was £50 each) and that was our shopping budget. It not only taught us how to budget and have a value for the money, it also kept us occupied and entertained while going shopping with her. So, from nine in the morning, when the shops would open, until the 5 p.m. closing, we were in the shops, stopping only briefly for lunch!
>
> Although my mother did love to shop, she was also obligated to do so since the choices in Iran were limited. On these trips, she not only had all her own wardrobe to fill for the year, but also orders from friends. Looking back, I'm surprised how she even managed. One of her main purchases was for fabric to have evening gowns and other dresses tailor-made back home for her.
>
> On Sundays, we would go sightseeing in London, and when weather permitted, picnicked at Hyde Park or Kew Garden, enjoying my mother's special delicious sandwiches. As time passed and it came closer to the end of the holidays, sadness loomed within our happy family unit. My mother would take us to Victoria Station, hug and kiss us as we said our goodbyes, and that familiar emptiness would find itself back in my stomach. Tears would flow and we would climb on the train to head back to school. Shortly thereafter I would get distracted with the excitement of being back with my friends and hearing them recount their exciting holidays.

With summer's approach, the weather improved in England, the daffodils and buttercups started to push themselves through the ground, days were longer and our free time was spent in the school grounds and garden. At the start of the summer term, uniforms were changed to a lighter, more cheerful fabric. With winter sports, netball and hockey, behind us, we looked forward to the field sports and tennis. I loved all the sports but was not particularly good at any of them. In the field sports, I was best at long-distance running and became a member of the relay team. All students were assigned to four different Houses, Sussex, Kent, Hampshire and Surrey. These Houses had a house captain, a vice captain, and a sports captain, chosen by the members of each House at the end of the year for the following year. We became dedicated to our Houses and competed amongst each other in matches. This built a strong team spirit, trained us for management, competition, leadership, responsibility and how to deal with hierarchy.

Then there was the end-of-year ritual of preparing for our departure. It was sad to be leaving our friends for the summer, but the excitement was palpable for most of us going back to the luxuries and comfort of our homes.

My life at boarding school, as described, repeated itself much the same way for six years until it was time for college. My sister left after five years to go to a finishing school in Lausanne, Switzerland, and later transferred to the American College of Switzerland. Again, I followed in her footsteps after completing my O-Levels.[3] The freedom I experienced for the first time, in the mountains of Switzerland, in a small school of 200 students where everyone became close friends, was exhilarating. My last thought was to study. It was heaven. I started dating for the first time, although it took me a few months to get the hang of it! My years at college opened space for freedom, skiing, discovering boys, falling in love and having fun. I graduated in three years in an effort to help my parents with the steep tuition of the college. Immediately after graduation, I headed for Johns Hopkins to study cytotechnology, following in the footsteps of my mother, fifteen years before me. After a year in the U.S., I returned to Iran and worked as a cytotechnologist at Tehran University. Three years later, I was married, after a courtship of only two months!

In sharing my story, I realized how embodied the memories of boarding school are for me and, more importantly, how I have kept in the forefront the positive ones, while letting go of the hardships and bad experiences. My attachment to my parents was always strong. Admittedly, being torn apart from them at a young age, for so many years, took a toll on me. Yet, I would not be the person I am now had I not gone through the experience of living away from them, outside my country. My father was a strict disciplinarian and this stern upbringing was deeply instilled in me. I did not dare do anything that disappointed my parents. Mrs Peck played only a small role in shaping my identity since, soon after my arrival at boarding school, she passed on the guardianship of my sister and me to her friend Mrs Richards. Mrs Richards simply arranged for our arrivals and departures to and from Iran. We were responsible for our own affairs. Making decisions and being expected to act as adults from an early age allowed me to become independent and able to adjust to living in different environments. After the Iranian Revolution, I lived in France for ten years with my family and now in the U.S., finally close to my parents, brother, my sister and her family. I have witnessed first hand the growth of my children as they have been embraced and nurtured by the love of my husband and me, and now look forward to sharing that love with my infant granddaughter as she begins her new life.

Notes

1. Namaz is the Muslim prayer carried out five times a day by the devout. On special occasions or in the mosque, an Imam or person of esteem traditionally guides the worshippers through the prayers.
2. The Latin word *exeat* (he/she may leave) is most commonly used in Britain describing a weekend absence from a centre of learning such as a boarding school.
3. The Ordinary Level General Certificate of Education (or 'O-Level') and Advanced Level Certificates ('A-Level') are the certification of completion given for each subject studied at the end of five years of secondary education in the British educational system.

2
IT WAS WHAT IT WAS

Fereshteh's story
The Grove School, Hindhead, Surrey (1974–1979)

'No daughter of ours can fail a school test'.

Fereshteh reflected on a single failure (*tajdidi*) at school in Tehran which, she believed, sealed her fate. The decision to send Fereshteh to England, along with three cousins, was made on a hot day at the family's summer home by the Caspian Sea,[1] where they had gathered for their annual vacation. She was twelve. Oblivious to everything else going on, that particular day, she was engaged with her newly discovered sense of womanhood. She was resting to calm her period pains, when the news of her imminent departure made its way through an open window of the living room. What was she to make of that?

Her aunt Sudi (Soosan's sister), who had previously spent her own adolescent years at boarding school, was asked to write a letter to her headmistress at The Grove School in Surrey, to seek admission for the upcoming academic year. In the meantime, the plan was for her to attend a summer school in Littlehampton, Sussex, to learn English.

In 1974, Fereshteh travelled to England with her grandmother and her male cousins, whose fate had been determined at the same time. That summer they were all sent to different schools. Subsequently, two of the boys went home only to return to England the following year.

> Summer school had the feel of a holiday camp by the seaside, so it should have been exciting. I didn't know English other than a few words, but I was learning the English ways and getting used to the food – or lack of it! We studied language in the mornings and went sightseeing in the afternoons. But even as a naive twelve-year-old Iranian, I vividly remember noticing how happy the English teacher and the wife of the housemaster were to see us off for the day so they could be alone with one another! During a visit years later, I found out that the couple had finally married after the housemaster's death.
>
> At the end of the summer, I returned to London to live with my grandmother, who had a flat in the city. By then I had a little more understanding of the English language so I wasn't afraid of feeling totally stupid when spoken to, but I still couldn't understand when people talked fast or how to interpret English mannerisms. Everything was a different experience, as were the people.
>
> The start of my new life at boarding school was looming and by now I was having enormous feelings of trepidation, but continued to simply assume my parents knew what was best for me. By that time, I had received The Grove School brochure and could at least see some pictures of the house, the grounds and the school where I was going to spend the next year. It looked unlike anywhere I had stayed before. My parents had never even seen the school – they just trusted that it would be perfect for me. A three-page list of required items had been sent to us, including everything from facial tissues to school uniforms! My grandmother and I made a trip to John Lewis, the assigned department store. The list seemed endless: bedding, toiletries, sewing

kit and so on, but the list of uniform items was even more intriguing: skirts and jackets, ties (What? I'm a girl!) cloak, rain coat, duffel coat, socks of all different heights and patterns, different sports gear for netball, hockey, tennis, rounders and swimming, shoes for this and that, 'Wellington boots' (What were they?) This was one thorough list! I had never bought so many things in one go, so it was exciting. Dutifully, we even bought a trunk that was on my list. How else was I to take everything with me? This was the English way to travel I thought.

In early September, my grandmother saw me off at Waterloo Station, where I was to take the coach to school. I am not sure whether I would have been more excited if I had believed that sending me to England was a result of an achievement rather than failure, but what I am sure about is that I believed I was going into a world beyond my imagination.

On arrival at school, the matrons and the headmistress greeted me at the main door. The school had its own grounds, chapel and gardens. It was undoubtedly beautiful, but I felt lost. At the time, I was the only foreigner at the school and everyone was kind to me. Groups of girls were chatting, catching up or getting to know each other. Though my English had improved, it was not enough. I was to share a room with three other girls. When we entered the room, they said: 'Bag this one'. I was still looking for the bags so I ended up with the bed nearest to the door with a tiny little cabinet by my side, where I lovingly placed the picture of my parents.

My first night felt a bit like being in prison. A stern-looking woman walked down the corridors with a huge bell in her hands, which she rung as if we were in the Middle Ages; this I soon understood meant that bedtime had begun. Pyjamas came out, slippers went on and, wash bags in hand, everyone queued for a sink. It took a while for me to sheepishly undress in front of the girls whilst they walked, fully naked, around me. This was a shock. We never undressed in front of anyone in Iran and I was immediately envious of the freedom and confidence the other girls felt.

Back home, I showered every day, but on the notice board I read that my bath days were fifteen minutes on Tuesdays, Thursdays and Saturdays with instructions on the amount of water allowed. Baths? I hadn't had one since I was a little girl playing swimming games with my tiny brother! I visited the bathroom and there was a hot and a cold tap but nothing to give me a mixture of both. How was that supposed to work? Swim in my own dirt and not rinse myself either? Thinking back, my bath times must have been hilarious to the daddy-long-legs who kept me company sitting on the windowsill: get in the bath quickly, wash, empty the bath then squat beside the taps, hands scooped under cold then hot water to splash myself. Having either burnt or frozen my skin several times, I quickly got the measurements right. My shopping priority became a showerhead at the earliest possible moment. The useless plastic showerhead was fun for the daddy-long-legs too! In 1975, to make matters worse, there was a nationwide drought and we were asked to share the bath water. This was just going too far! With a polite smile, I often managed to dodge that situation.

It took me a while to get over the shock of breakfast, where girls seemed to stuff themselves as if they weren't going to eat again. But then, this was also the case for lunch, tea and supper. By the end of the year you could see I had also taken to their way of thinking (or rather eating) as, in my father's words, I'd turned into a balloon!

For a long time, I didn't know what we were doing in class. Luckily, just like all those different items of clothing, we had different coloured books for each subject. So, I hid my ignorance by copying the other girls and taking out whatever colour book they did. The whole thing felt like a long, drawn out punishment. I had failed in English when in Iran, but now I couldn't even understand the other subjects, even the ones I was good at. At times, I just stared at the board with tears rolling down my face. I felt stupid. The teachers were very kind, patient and discreet about this. I liked this English way. Back home the corner street shop owners would have known if I'd cried in my chemistry class!

Today, Fereshteh is a beautiful, gentle, thoughtful soul. It is almost painful to imagine her, wandering, lost, at the age of twelve, in strange surroundings believing she was being punished. In the absence of a fluent language or understanding of her situation, how did she make it through those days? How did she relate to other girls? Or did she?

The path to school from our boarding house was called 'the rhododendron walk'. We took this path every day at 8.15 a.m. after breakfast. Dressed in the appropriate uniform and with a tie around my neck, I walked alongside some girls making fun of the two in front who were walking shoulder-to-shoulder, calling them 'lesbians'. I decided the idea of walking with a friend hand-in-hand was never going to happen here as it did in my school playgrounds in Tehran. I became very aware of how I behaved and the physical distance I kept with others.

In my first week at school I was somehow drawn into a secret meeting; I couldn't understand what was going on but there was a heated conversation and whispers about bringing a torch and something warm to the window at midnight. Was this an expedition? There was a vote and I put my hand up too. At 11.50 p.m., the girl who took me to the meeting came to collect me. We crept down the staircase where girls were climbing out the window into darkness. At the last minute, the leader of the team told me to go back to bed. I don't know if she felt responsible for me or thought that I would have held them back. The next morning there was a huge drama as the school realized that the girls had run away in protest against the new headmistress. Police found them after a few days. Needless to say, they were punished heavily on their return. To think I could have been expelled so soon after my arrival would have been a funny outcome!

The other awkward thing was the bodily noises the girls freely made. Back in Tehran, people left the room if they wanted to blow their noses, but here they readily burped, farted and repeatedly blew huge amounts of snot into their handkerchiefs. Not me. Never in public and never in my John Lewis handkerchief from the list! Now I am comfortable with all that, having lived in England for the last forty years!

Fereshteh's overall reaction to the boarding school experience is mixed.

The first year was the best. The girls in my room were lovely. They would dare each other to run naked round the room. They never asked me to do so, though secretly I wished they would or that I could. I did take on 'dares' such as screaming out the window or running down the corridors after lights out. The matron always punished the other girls but not me. Everyone was kind to me. Yet secretly I wanted to be punished like them. I always smiled at everyone so at the end of the year when they gave prizes out I received one for posture and smiling! Not much of an achievement after a year's exile, but I was happy.

I missed my parents immensely. I always carried a picture of them in my pocket, even when I changed from uniform to sports gear. I spoke to them occasionally, but we had a limited number of minutes to talk on the phone. It wasn't easy. I remember writing a letter and saying: 'I am only twelve and I need my parents. I want to come back'. There was no one to guide me so I just went along and followed the rules.

A year later in 1975, I returned to Iran to continue my education. I had learned to speak English by then, which seemed to have been the objective! I went back to my old school and made new friends. I was popular and trendy because I had returned from England! I had also learned German at school and wanted to speak it, so my father promised that as a reward, if I did well in school that year, he would send me to a German summer school this time.

Whilst in Hamburg, Germany for the summer, I received a letter from my parents about plans for us to immigrate to England as a family. At that time, moving from country to country was not as difficult or challenging as it has become since the 1979 revolution. So once again, I went straight from Hamburg back to The Grove School. My younger brother was sent to a weekly boarding school and my mother, who had accompanied him, stayed in the flat in London. For reasons unknown to me, by Christmas my parents decided against moving to London. They said it was too late to take me out of school and back into one in Tehran. Again, though I was very upset, I didn't question their decision. So, my brother and I stayed behind, he in London and me in Hindhead, Surrey. By now, I had two cousins and a brother in the U.K. We were all placed in different counties and hardly saw each other except during the holidays when we all gathered at my grandmother's.

On my return to The Grove School, things had changed. There were other foreign girls, from Nigeria and China. This was great. I was happy when an Iranian friend of my aunt sent her daughter to our school and I was asked to take care of her. But our friendship soon grew cold. I couldn't understand her mannerisms.

Luckily, I don't remember the bad times.

For me, boarding school was fun. I learned about English culture and history. It was a regimented culture. On Sundays, we went to church. Other foreign girls refused to go, but I loved it. Singing hymns made me emotional, as it was the only place I could cry for missing something – although I am not sure what or who anymore. Just missing.

Because of my summer in Hamburg, which had helped with my German, I was promoted to the A-Level German class. This was a big achievement for me. I helped all the girls with their O-Level German. My dream was to become an interpreter at the United Nations. I'd found French hard but was excited to go to Switzerland to study it and maybe Italian too! I mentioned my dream to my parents, but it was never taken seriously or talked about. Having a career was never expected of the teachers didn't expect us to be anything either. My parents were not familiar with the British education system, so I had no guidance as to what subjects to take for my O-Levels. I just followed what my friends did. If they dropped a subject, so did I. I can never forget how easy it was to drop biology. When asked by the headmistress why, I simply said I don't like it and she signed me off. I had no idea how important a subject such as biology was and how limited in life I would be without it. It never occurred to me to ask my parents and, obviously, there was no communication between them and the school. I was expected to be in charge of my own life, so if I failed in my courses, this time I wasn't going to let them know.

You know, it wasn't so much the boarding school that was a problem; it was more the lack of parenting. I think the whole experience could have been managed differently. In those days, parents trusted the system, especially the English system. Now I think 'It was what it was', it was perhaps the thing to do and I am who I am as a result. I certainly wouldn't want to be anyone else.

It's difficult to say whether I was isolated from family and friends or whether I segregated myself, but the positive outcome is that I became self-reliant. I saw my family once a year on holidays. Although I was growing up, I always seemed to be the 'twelve-year-old' when I returned home. My parents, who had almost no idea of what my life was like in England, would suddenly become argumentative over a short skirt and my everyday conduct.

When I had my son, I tried to compensate for everything I'd missed, perhaps too much! I looked at my son at twelve and thought, he is so young to know what to do for the rest of his life, remembering those years of feeling lost. I talked to him all the time, asking about his wishes and desires, failures and accomplishments; I still do. He knows he can share them all with me. I guess parenting has changed; life wasn't as tough for young adults as it is now.

I returned to Iran after my A-Levels. The Iran/Iraq war,[2] which had started in 1980 had made travel difficult and I became stuck there for some time. In hindsight, those two years were the best years with my family. There were no expectations of me. I made new friends, learned to draw, paint, read poetry, ski, laugh. I took the opportunity to work with my father in his surgery to be close to him and to learn about his practice. While I appreciated the education and experiences I had in the U.K., being back in Iran was a kind of reconciliation. It grounded me and reminded me of who I was and what a rich culture I was born into. During those two years, I got to know my parents as individuals, especially my father, to whom I became very attached. I was also able to build a relationship with my new-born brother. I concluded that my parents' actions were because they believed it was the best for me. They too had made sacrifices. They had lost me and now they had found me again. After the borders opened, now stronger and with more backbone and determination, it was my time to fight to return to England. I wanted to become someone useful.

Gathering her thoughts and after what seems a reflective moment, she continues with a contagious, sarcastic laugh:

Now, I am a bloody independent fifty-one-year-old. Being too independent means you don't let anyone in, you learn to look after yourself, you don't let yourself fall because there might be no one to hold you up. If you do, you don't let anyone see you fall or give you a hand. I absolutely love what I do now, I feel lucky to do what gives me so much pleasure and that means I can carry on learning for the rest of my life. Of course, there is a price to pay for being stoic and self-sufficient, but that'll be the topic for your next book!

I love my parents and, now a parent of a young adult myself, know how sad it was not having me close to them; so, I am more aware of the sacrifices my parents made for what they thought was best for me.

Fereshteh was about to end her story when she seemed to remember something else, wondering whether she should talk about it and whether it was relevant to the subject matter.

Did I tell you about …?

Once, when I was at my grandmother's, my friend's father (of the Iranian girl at my school) came to visit. I was alone. He insisted on coming in. He began sexually harassing me; his hands were all over me. I was running around the flat to get away from him. I couldn't tell anyone. I don't know why, perhaps because he was a family friend I didn't want to cause trouble for anyone, especially my friend. Finally, he left some money on the table and told me not to tell. I didn't confess to this until years later after he had passed away! Then I told my aunt.

Fereshteh's earlier description of the 'awkward' relationship with her Iranian friend at boarding school now made sense!

After her return to London, Fereshteh was educated as an interior designer. A few years later, she partnered with her then Italian husband to run a successful architectural practice while she became a lecturer at a university. After the breakup of her marriage, she continued as a lecturer at Kingston and Chelsea College of Art and Design whilst taking care of her son. Disillusioned with educational bureaucracy and exhausted from being a working single mother, following a long illness, she decided to change her career and returned to school. Today, she is a successful Five Element acupuncturist with a well-established practice in London.

Notes

1 Caspian Sea, the largest inland body of water located between Europe and Iran, borders northwestern Iran, Afghanistan, Kurdemnistan, Russia, Kazakhstan and Azerbaijan. 'Shomal' (literally meaning North in Farsi), as most Iranians affectionately refer to the Caspian Sea, was, and continues to be, the most frequent vacation destination for families living in Tehran.
2 The Iran/Iraq War started after the 1979 Revolution in September 1980 and lasted for eight years.

3
THIS TOO SHALL PASS

Azy's story
Charters Towers School, Bexhill-on-Sea, Sussex (1965–1969)

Azy came to Charters Towers a year after Roya and Shirley and at the same time as Roxane (Chapter 8). They were welcomed into the small unit of the Iranian classmates. The four soon became inseparable, especially Azy and Shirley, who soon discovered that they shared a rebellious spirit and would often get into trouble resisting the discipline and the system. Azy shared her story with Roya in a hotel room in Los Angeles where they met for this interview.

> I was fourteen when I went to boarding school. My parents came to this decision because my uncle's wife had attended Charters Towers a few years earlier. First, I was sent and then two years later my sister, Heidi, joined me. I felt very lonely at first. I didn't know the language and although there were other Iranian girls at the school, I felt isolated. At home, we were always with family and not with friends so I was not familiar with the art of making friends.
>
> Mrs Thomson, my guardian, had been recommended to my father by his close friend, Shirley's father, although I didn't know Shirley before school. The first time I went to England my father accompanied me. Unlike other girls, I rarely spent any vacation in a holiday home. Usually, my parents would come to London and we would travel to Switzerland or France, or I would go back to Iran.
>
> I remember my first night in the dorm. I was sleeping in my bed and saw girls moving into each other's beds. I was petrified but curious as to what was going on. It just seemed totally weird that someone would join someone else in their bed. I remember thinking that they too must be lonely to need to hold and comfort each other. Of course, later I realized that this was not only to alleviate their loneliness, but that the girls were simply experimenting and discovering their sexual desires with another person. The Iranian girls were much more reserved, since for young girls in Iran, sexuality was frowned upon and not expressed publicly. The 'Western' girls were much more expressive and open about their physical needs.
>
> It bothered me that I couldn't understand the language and I was behind the others in class, so I learned English very quickly. At night, with the use of a flashlight, I would take my books into the bathroom and review for hours everything that the rest of my class had studied that day. In the first year, I succeeded at being at the top of my class in chemistry and physics. I have always had a competitive nature and hate being at the bottom of anything.
>
> I don't have much memory of the school or the teachers, but I remember Miss McGarry, the headmistress, and Madam, her mother, who taught us English. I hated the school so much and tried not to get too involved, thinking this would be my shield against the school. I felt that if I was defiant and broke every rule I could, I would prove that they had no power over me. For example, our socks had to be below our knees. So, every morning when I got dressed I made sure that my socks were not where they were supposed to be. My hair was always a mess and Miss McGarry was always telling me off.

I really enjoyed getting her angry. I am not confrontational but if someone gets on my bad side there is no way I will let them win! I loved my classes but I remember I would wake up in the morning thinking about how I could demonstrate my hatred of this place that day. It felt like the day was not right if I didn't get any of the teachers mad at me! Every day it seemed my goal was to get on Miss McGarry's nerves! I was not scared of her like the other girls, but I made her the symbol of my misery. My aim was to break her. I couldn't show anger to anyone else so my anger was focused on her.

How did boarding school affect me? The effect was that it gave me a self-made armour. In Iran, I wasn't used to rules and regulations like most other girls. My leadership qualities were born at boarding school mainly because of my defiant behaviour. I never liked rules. Rules, such as getting up at a certain time in the morning or making our beds a certain way, bothered me. I believed that rules were for stupid people who had to be told what to do and how to get from A to B. I didn't want to be part of that system. My character changed as a result of boarding school. It became hard for me to trust many people or open up and show my vulnerabilities. I witnessed the bitchiness of young girls at boarding school and how they were friends one day and then talked behind each other's back the next. This taught me to stay closed and share my secrets with only a deserving few in my life. I became a total introvert. I had a few Iranian friends in my class and remember a few others at school, including a couple of girls from Portugal – Theresa and Louise are names that come to me.

Despite my mother's detachment and lack of involvement in our lives, I was brought up in a very loving atmosphere at home. I had a grandfather who was a saint and loved me dearly. When I was sick he would stay up all night by my bed to watch over me. When my parents were travelling, I stayed at my grandparents' house. He went as far as to check our poop to make sure it was healthy. I do the same with my grandchildren today! I came from that loving, trusting home atmosphere to this school. So, I became a fighter. When I want something and make up my mind to get it, I go after it. The experience of boarding school gave me the strength to get through the revolution in Iran. Had I not had that experience, I believe the revolution would have destroyed me. I lived in a very protective environment in Iran. Everyone stayed within the circle of aunts, uncles and cousins. As a result, I am very close to all my cousins to this day. Before I went to England, we used to spend every weekend in a family member's house. I had never even been to a store while in Iran. But because of my boarding school experience, I was the only person in the family who had friends outside of our family circle. Without my friends, I wouldn't have known how to cope during the revolution when families were broken up and migrated to different countries.

My family was one of the wealthiest families in Iran. Our driver literally dropped us off by the steps of the plane when we were travelling. But once the revolution happened, we had to leave Iran with very little money.

With my husband and my daughter, we ended up living at my parents' one-bedroom apartment for a while when we first moved to the U.S. The building didn't allow children, so we slept in the closet and had to hide my one-year-old daughter. But boarding school had prepared me for this unfamiliar life and taught me that I could cope and survive anything.

My mother was not one to show emotion and was uninvolved in my schooling. That was my grandfather's job. I didn't miss her much, but I remember when my father left me at school, I thought to myself, 'Oh my God! Now I'm alone'. I felt lost and deserted. I'm very good at not showing emotion; now that I think of it, I guess I get that from my mother. I remember seeing you (Roya) and Shirley. I was very wary of you, but Shirley had an inviting smile and I felt like I had a comrade in her. This turned out to be exactly right because she had the same defiant reaction to the rules that I had.

What I enjoyed most at school was the thick bread with butter and honey, my favourite part of breakfast. I loved brussels sprouts, but often intentionally dropped them on the floor so that I would be told off. The food wasn't that good. I do remember our midnight feasts and how Shirley and I would arrange them. We would go to town on Saturday and, because we had more pocket money than the rest of the group, we would buy everything that we could think of and invite our friends to join.

The most memorable times for me at school were when I was being defiant. I loved getting Miss McGarry mad at me. I remember how Shirley and I made a mockery of her system of leadership with the assignments of house captains and vice captains. I realized I had a power to have an impact on others; I was a leader. I also realized that I could destroy this woman who everyone feared; even the smell of her perfume would make people fearful of her presence. She was so rigid; you can't be taking care of kids and be so inflexible. She didn't like any of the girls and she should never have been an educator. She should have never been in a position to influence young minds because she destroyed them. In contrast, her mother, Madame, was a loving, caring individual. I still remember the kindness in her face. All the foreign students were assigned to Madam's English language class. She taught us in small groups of no more than three in her office. Like Miss McGarry, she was always well dressed and coiffed, but unlike Miss McGarry, her presence provided us comfort and encouragement. Madam was old, had white hair and suffered from Parkinson's disease, which caused her hands to shake incessantly, but she prided herself on her most important lesson, which was handwriting.

My defiance of the system continued to my own detriment at times, as I was punished often. We were required to wear our hats when we were outside but I had to be reminded twenty times to put mine back on. I would take it off as soon as the teachers turned their back. When it was time for our O-Levels, Shirley and I decided we weren't going to study. While others studied, we played around. So, the result was that we managed to fail most of our O-Levels! I passed maths and Persian but had to stay for an extra term and redo the rest. The second time I passed all of them since I had set my mind to it.

Now that I think back, boarding school was such an amazing experience that despite my resistance, prepared me for the unexpected changing lifestyle that was in my future. It helped me cope with my post-revolution life so much better than I would have managed otherwise. I learned that I didn't need anyone to survive. I would have never known this had I not had that experience in my formative years.

Azy's guardian was one of the most influential people in her life. She goes on to explain why:

Mrs Thomson was a lovely woman and became my role model. She lived in Brighton and every mid-term holiday I stayed with her. Shirley's sister would pick us up from school to accompany Shirley to London and drop me off in Brighton on their way. I vividly remember Mrs Thomson bringing me a cup of tea and milk to my bed in the morning. She also taught me how to bake and I continue to love to cook and bake. There were always three or four other girls and boys who stayed with Mrs Thomson, but I didn't bond with any of them. I bonded with her because for the first time I saw what it was to be a nurturing mother. My grandmother and mother were not maternal, so I must have learned these qualities from Mrs Thomson. My grandfather had showed me love and affection but that was through a man's perspective; I had never experienced a woman's care. I didn't want to be anything like my mother. I observed the way Mrs Thomson was with her own children. In the afternoon, she would make us Marmite sandwiches, would sit us down, sing and play games with us. I remember spending Easter with her and going on an Easter egg hunt. I never spent Christmas with the family, though. I continued to be in contact with Mrs Thomson for a while after I went back to Iran, but eventually lost touch completely with her.

There was no good reason for my parents to send us away, other than it was fashionable at the time. I don't think my parents ever took us children into consideration when we were growing up. My grandfather did. He adored us. It seems that once my parents were married they were expected to have children so they did, but they had no idea what it meant to be a caring parent. Unconditional love wasn't part of the equation for them. Neither of my parents was emotionally expressive. My father didn't know any better and my mother was very self-absorbed. I felt unloved. Now I understand that many women have kids but don't necessarily have maternal instincts. My mother was only sixteen when I was born.

It was upsetting for me being separated from my grandfather. He was really my caregiver. I don't think my relationship with my parents would have been any different had I not gone to boarding school. I don't have much respect for people who wait for handouts or feel entitled. My father worked for my grandfather and, although he worked hard, his success was due to my grandfather. I never respected my parents. My grandfather was my role model. To this day, his picture is on my computer and I talk to him and ask him for guidance and protection. If I want to make a major decision, I always think about how he would act and what decision he would make.

Azy's grandfather was a successful businessman and a well-known industrialist, hence a respected figure in the business community of Iran. He was a religious and spiritual man who influenced Azy's spirituality and religious beliefs. She believes that he is her guardian angel, always with her, guiding and mentoring her. Azy claims that she doesn't dwell on negativity in her life and given the unpleasantness of her school years, struggles to recall the memories.

> These are the years that I really want to put behind me. And yet I can't help but believe it was a good experience and that there was a reason we were sent away. It taught me how to survive and deal with stress. I spent so many years of my life dealing with the stress of growing my business. I would wake up in the middle of the night with the anxiety of how to pay the rent the next month. It was outrageous. Or waking up at two in the morning because someone has broken into the warehouse is not fun. Working seriously for serious earnings is not fun! I don't think anyone would choose to work if they didn't have to pay the bills. There are so many other things you can do in life if you have money. I don't believe I would have chosen to work like I did if it wasn't for the need to maintain a certain lifestyle.
>
> I tried to have as much fun as I could at school. The friendships I have with you and Shirley have stayed to this day. We bonded after my initial hostility towards you (Roya) and I then trusted you. Trust continues to be difficult for me to this day, although it is one of the most important values for me. I remember your parents would write letters to you in Farsi. Because your Farsi wasn't good, you would ask me to read them to you! My Farsi wasn't that good either, so I would read a few words and make up the rest. I didn't receive many letters myself, although I had to write home every Sunday. Unfortunately, as a result of the little practice I had, I didn't keep my Farsi language and lost my reading and writing capabilities too.
>
> At the start of the summer holidays, we travelled by train to London and I would then get myself on the plane to Tehran. It was a much safer world then. Girls at eighteen were old enough to get married so at twelve or thirteen we were treated as grownups. We stayed alone in hotels and did our shopping alone before travelling back home.
>
> I felt responsible for protecting my siblings. My sister (three years younger) was miserable at home without me, alone with my mom. I believed that if my sister came to England, I could protect her. So, when she finally arrived, she became like my child. She always says that I was her real mother. When my

brother (five years younger) came to England for boarding school, I became his guardian. If he were travelling, I would pick him up from the train and take him to the airport.

I have a fear of vulnerability and suppress my emotions. The only people for whom I have unconditional raw feelings are my two kids. I have never really been in love with anyone because I never wanted to feel vulnerable. If I ever felt like I was getting too close to anyone, I would break off the relationship for fear of being hurt. I trust you, Shirley and my sister implicitly. I will share my secrets, but I will not be emotional in front of anyone. I don't feel the need to get too close to anyone else. I have good friends that I trust and I have great kids. I don't even recognize that I may need help to ask for it. I believe I can do it all myself. I don't expect anyone to do anything for me.

After many years of post-revolution hardship, Azy launched several very successful food distribution companies with the help of her husband, father and uncle. As chief executive, she expanded this company to a multi-million-dollar enterprise. When Azy was running her business, she worked from dawn until late at night, six days a week. Ironically, it was Azy's mother who took care of the children in her absence. By the time she sold her business, it had multiplied many fold, but at the high cost to her health and quality of life. She retired from work at a fairly young age but managed to accumulate enough wealth to allow her and her family to live comfortably again.

I have a mind of my own. In my business, I listened to the management but ultimately trusted my own intuition and actions. I knew I had to make sure that I didn't miss anything through their conversations, but I always believed the solution would come to me and that has always worked for me. However, what I know now is making decisions alone can be lonely and get overwhelming, which is why I decided to finally sell the business. It got to the point where the business had grown so much that it was too difficult for me to handle on my own. Perhaps it was because other people in management were not doing their job correctly, but I realized that I had reached my full capacity. I knew what had to be done but I didn't have the guts to replace them and I couldn't bring myself to ask for help. I decided that I should just get out of the business and felt forced into selling the company. In retrospect, it was a good decision, although it didn't seem so at the time.

The experience of boarding school gave me the ability to run a large organization and make it successful. It taught me to ask myself 'What's the worst-case scenario?' in any major decision I make and then go from there. I remember when I first went to Charters Towers I felt abandoned and was especially upset with my grandfather. I couldn't believe he would allow this to happen to me. Then I thought to myself 'What is the worst that can happen and can I manage that worst-case scenario?' If I can manage it, I go for it.

My aim in life was to enjoy myself. I could have gone to any university in England or the U.S., but I chose the best 'fun' school, which was the American College of Switzerland. Much like the rest of the women in my family, I wasn't brought up wanting to earn a living, so I thought why not use this time to have fun. My general outlook on life is that 'it will pass'. I have a beautiful painting in my kitchen – of a mirror that has been shattered – and there is a quote 'this too shall pass', so I always believe things will get better.

The only support system I had at school was having my two best friends. I didn't have any other friends. And yet, I never had any self-esteem issues as I trusted myself. I was very competitive. My biggest challenge was to learn English and be the best in the class. I realized from an early age that I have a photographic memory and never needed to study, but I never missed a class, even in college. I knew that the only learning I would be getting would be while I was attending class. I have attention deficit disorder so I can't concentrate on one topic for a long period of time. That's why I was so successful in my business. I was at my peak when I was multitasking: handling two phones simultaneously, as well as having someone in my office and someone waiting outside my door; I didn't have to concentrate too long on one thing. That is how my mind works.

Attention Deficit Hyperactivity Disorder (ADHD) previously known as Attention Deficit Disorder (ADD) affects many children who carry the symptoms into adulthood. During the 1970s this and many other psychological states were unknown and typically went undiagnosed. Children with ADHD were often thought to be lazy or troublemakers, both being justifiably punishable.

I was never a high achiever. I would have loved to stay at home and be with my kids and spend their growing years with them. That's why now I value being at home with my four grandchildren taking care of them. People who don't know me well are surprised at this new role of grandmother that I have taken on for myself. The first impression I generally give to others is that I am harsh, even though I try to show my real softer side. My daughter even warned her boyfriend not to be scared of me when he first met me! Later he said that if it weren't for my sister Heidi's presence he would have walked away saying, 'I don't want to deal with a mother-in-law like this'. Now he adores me.

My purpose in working hard to be successful was that I wanted my children to grow up with the same lifestyle I had enjoyed. I never wanted them to worry about money. I am extremely close with both of my children who now live within a few miles of me and have become successful professionals in their own rights.

Now, I am finally enjoying my life. I don't put much value on what people think and I do things that I want to do and don't do things that don't interest me. People are not that important to me. I went through the revolution with the armour of having gone to boarding school. If I put my mind to it, I can do whatever I want. I believe that without that experience, none of this would have happened. I would have been destroyed, like many others in my family. The only person who managed to pull him or herself out was me, and I pulled my family up with me. It brought out qualities in me that have even surprised me. I would have been living in a utopia, being useless and just spending money. Emotionally, it has been bad because had I experienced love growing up, perhaps I would not have been so harsh on myself and on the people around me. I admit that I was very strict with my kids. My motto was if I am doing my best you better be doing your best. A 'B' was not acceptable in our household. Thank God, my kids were bright. If they hadn't been, I can't imagine the pressure it would have been on them. Failure was never an option. I don't believe I was a great mother because of this.

I became a philanthropist in the latter years of running my business because of my faith. I felt I had to pay back for all that had been given to me. I was brought up in a religious environment. My grandfather was a big philanthropist and I learned from him. I established a foundation, the Iranian Scholarship Fund, which provides full college scholarship for outstanding Iranian students who cannot afford the U.S. college tuitions. I also founded a senior living facility for Iranians where seniors can enjoy residential assisted care with minimum payment. I also sit on the board of many philanthropic organizations. I never say 'no' to anyone who reaches out to me if I think it is for a good cause. It is a way for me to express my gratitude to God. I think my success was not because I am super intelligent. I believe some of it is luck and my belief that God has had his hand in my life, helping me through it all. I am not an institutionally religious person but I am spiritual and have a lot of faith.

Azy now lives in the San Francisco Bay area, surrounded by her family, spending her time taking care of her grandchildren and engaging in her philanthropic work.

SUMMARY

We began with the stories of Roya, Fereshteh and Azy, who each described a unique experience, providing a snapshot of how their lives were shaped as they embarked on their voyage to a British boarding school. The stories exemplify the notion of parental privilege when it came to making life-shaping decisions for their daughters.

Their parents trusted the system they were placing their daughters into without question. In some ways, they let go of their own responsibilities while continuing to lead their own busy and somewhat elitist lives. It seemed that as long as someone knew of a school and another had sent their child, it was a good enough decision for them to do so too. If one child was sent then the others were to follow in an attempt at fairness, regardless of the individual child's pedagogic requirements. The girls did not question the decision that was made for them assuming that 'father knows best'. During their regular returns to Iran, in the proximity of their parents, they became the little Persian girls who followed the expectations and authority of their parents and behaved accordingly, giving up the very liberties they had become accustomed to in England. For the most part, as women, they do not blame their parents for the choices that were made even as their parents' rationale for doing so continues to evade their understanding.

Roya's story provides a detailed picture of life at boarding school, but it is a narrative that conveys the total subjugation of a young girl to the wishes of her father, whose goal was to keep her under control. Roya's father, a well-known physician in Tehran, was among the strict secular fathers who worried about his professional reputation, as well as the reputation of his two daughters. Keeping the girls under strict supervision is a cultural theme that is repeated in many of the stories, though each girl reacts differently to this authority based on her own personality and the moral values of her family. Distanced from loved ones prematurely, Roya experiences conflicting feelings of separation anxiety and calming nostalgia about her past. The pain of separation experienced at a young age lingers vividly in Roya's memory, as it continues to impact her life today.

For Fereshteh, whose father was a quiet-mannered dentist, his silence spoke louder than words. Her story is an acknowledgement that there was no room for questioning her parent's decision then and that now there is only room for understanding and acceptance. The idea of attending boarding school was not new in Fereshteh's extended family, but her particular path was determined as the result of a regular family meeting that did not include her and was perceived as a punishment for failing a course. Letting go of her adolescent dream and hope for a career as a United Nations interpreter, she continued to trust in her parent's will, while leading a life at the cross section of conformity and rebellion.

Azy's narrative begins to tell the story of how other women influenced the girls' psychological development and shaped their upbringing. In the absence of the love of a nurturing mother or grandmother, Azy found the compassion and care she was looking for in Mrs Thomson, spending many holidays at the 'loving woman's' home. Mrs Thomson's positive relationship with her own children, as well as other children who boarded at her house, became Azy's image of a loving mother. Disconnected from the influence and daily guidance of parents, she finds a surrogate as her guide and mentor as she grows up to become a successful business woman and a nurturing and loving mother.

While they cannot envision what could have been the outcome of their lives had they not been sent away, Roya, Fereshteh and Azy acknowledge the instant need for mandatory maturity beyond their early years, forced to become independent leaders and fighters with a deep sense of responsibility. Had they lived in the privileged, abundant environment of their home, would they have expanded on these qualities?

PART II
A life lived

INTRODUCTION

The ache for home lives in all of us, the safe place where we can go as we are and not be questioned.

Maya Angelou[1]

As Iranians, we are a generation of women whose life experiences as young girls were and remain inconceivable to many, in particular, women in today's Iran. We were the children of the privileged-class families, rich and educated, with parents who had already been exposed to and, in some ways, had embraced the Western culture. The social class distinction and the surging discontent in Iran was salient in the 1970s but we, as children of the privileged, were oblivious to the lives of the majority of Iranians, who lived austere lives and struggled with societal class mobility. To some extent, the Islamic Revolution had sprung upon the likes of us because we had been so sheltered. Except for our relationships with the house help, the 'Rasoulis' of Roya's (Chapter 1) world or the driver who would keep his shock in check as he watched her run in the streets of Tehran in her short tennis skirt, we had little connection with people from other classes of society. Our lifestyle was alien to a large section of the population that, for all intents and purposes, found it unattainable, perhaps enviable and arguably immoral.

We were given the opportunity of boarding school not available to many women before us; 'opportunities' that few of our own mothers had benefited from and, ironically, opportunities that we would be hard pressed to bestow on our own daughters. Our mothers had, for the most part, lived in the shadows of their fathers or husbands with little attention to their own inner child, intellect or abilities. Except for Roya's mother who was a professional, our mothers, though mostly educated, were stay-at-home moms. We too, though educated by the best, were expected to practice a similar set of behaviours shaped by the traditional view of women in the U.K. in the 1960s and augmented by the rigid view of women in the Iranian culture. We were measured on how 'good' we were as daughters, while we measure our own daughters on who they want to be. As mothers, we encourage our daughters to believe that they can do whatever they set their minds to do. Our daughters are independent thinkers; the beneficiaries of a different world, one in which standing on the shoulder of women before them, they can now define their own role and place in society, as they bridge their heritage, Iranian cultural demands, with the Western expressions of their identity. Is it a surprise then, that despite proclaimed advantages of our boarding school education, we believe that separation from a parent at an early age is unnatural and that none of us were prepared to send our own children to boarding school?

From the moment we stepped foot on that giant airplane full of strangers, or arrived at the front door of our selected schools, we were alone. We were fenced from the world in general, and men in particular, as we entered the predominantly female space that was to prepare us for life as a wife and a mother. All at once, the little 'good girl', who was nurtured and protected by her parents, had no choice but to move into a life mode of survival, responsibility and premature adulthood, to be strong, not to cry or complain. Informed by feminist geographer McDowell (1999),[2] Spencer (2013)[3] frames boarding schools as a blurred physical and psychic space where the students are neither children nor adults. And so it was, for many of us as children, that it became our *modus operandi* to conquer hardships at school, both to meet our obligation to our parents and to prove our worthiness of being granted the privilege of boarding school! We met the expectations of the grownups the only way we knew how; doing our best and as Churchill would say – 'to keep buggering on'. Away from home, in the absence of immediate loving care, we hid our natural childhood yearning for such presence. We adapted to and, at times, rebelled against the demands of our school authorities, but our ultimate goal was to make our parents proud. We mostly succeeded in doing so, sometimes at a cost to our personal well-being.

Carol Gilligan's (1982)[4] well-known work on the psychology of women suggests that adolescence is often a time of disconnection, perhaps dissociation or repression in a woman's life. Often, we do not remember, select to forget or cover up what we may have experienced at that age. In our stories, there are those of us who hold on to our voice not to risk disruption to our way of life, keeping feelings hidden, buried as we did during our adolescence. Then, empowered by our all-female surroundings, we satisfied our urge for both intimacy and individuality through the generally acceptable adolescent 'crush', which provided an outlet for emotional expression and allowed for experiencing an idealistic feeling of love. By the time we entered the real world of gender diversity, we had learned greater self-control and protected ourselves by maintaining distance with others as in Gilligan's (1982) words 'sexual and emotional satisfaction shifted away from familial models toward individual discipline' (p. 605) and as we searched for a greater sense of self-respect and power.

We did not come from abusive or dysfunctional families, but this pattern of sending children away seems to expose much about the structure of our families, the nature of our parents' marriage(s), their commitment to the development of their children and their expectations of us as children. Our ambivalence towards the root of their decision lies in our lack of answers to questions we have as adults. Were they cognizant of the burden of responsibility placed on us? On our older siblings? Were they aware of our yearning for love? Was sending all the children away for better education, as opposed to just one child, their attempt at being fair? Other than financing our education, what role did they presume to play in our upbringing? Did they love us? Did they send us away to punish us, because we were not 'good'? Were they getting rid of us so that they could live their lives free of the responsibilities of parenthood? How did they define what was best for us?

The following stories continue to highlight similar questions about our upbringing and key social and cultural practices among our families.

Notes

1 Angelou, M. (1986), *All God's Children Need Travelling Shoes*, Random House, New York.
2 McDowell, L. (1999), *Gender, Identity and Place: Understanding Feminist Geographies*, University of Minnesota Press, Minneapolis, Minnesota.
3 Spencer, S. (2013), Boarding school fictions: schoolgirls' own communities of learning. *Women's History Review* 22(3), 386–402.
4 Gilligan C. (1982), *In a Different Voice: Psychological Theory and Women's Development*, Harvard University Press, Cambridge, Massachusetts.

4
SAGHI OR SALLY?

Saghi's story

Moira House, Eastbourne, Sussex (1973–1975)
Chateaubriand School, Cannes, France (1975–1977)

Roya and Saghi met in 1992 in the elevator of Roya's parents' apartment in Chevy Chase, Maryland. Saghi, a tall, stunning young lady with an infectious smile, appeared approachable and friendly. Roya was instantly drawn to her and intrigued by her presence. In the years to come, they often ran into each other where they exchanged niceties until later when they met at a party and, for the first time, had a conversation. They have been friends ever since. When Saghi heard about this book, she revealed to Roya that she too was the product of a British boarding school and agreed to share her story.

> The decision to send me to England was made, first, because it was the thing to do for a better education at the time and, I believe, because my parents wanted the best for their children. Second, I believe it was convenient for them to have the children away as they lived their young lives together. This was the second marriage for both of them and they enjoyed to party in their own way. My brothers and sister, who were about eight to ten years older than me, were already finishing their education in England. I was the baby of the family. My father had an older son and daughter from a previous marriage and my mother, a son from her first husband.
>
> After finishing fifth grade in Iran, my mom and dad decided to take a road trip with me to visit my siblings in England. They were an adventurous couple. We climbed into our orange Peykan Javanan[1] and started driving towards England! I remember the trip vividly. I can visualize that moment as we were driving away from our house and looking back from the rear-view window, to see the remaining family holding the tray with the traditional bowl of water and a copy of the Quran.[2] As a ritual, we had passed under the tray for safe keeping, before climbing into the car. This ritual was not a religious practice, although it has religious connotations, but one that was a tradition in most Iranian families before venturing out on a long trip.
>
> The journey took about one month as we visited many different countries and experienced a variety of adventures on the way. First, we stopped in Turkey and travelled on the ferry for three days crossing the Black Sea. I threw up incessantly because I had eaten some Macadamia nuts just before embarking on the ferry. In Turkey, coming back from lunch one day we lost our car, only to eventually find it under a pile of spectators fascinated by this Iranian-made orange vehicle. In Germany, one night we got lost on our way to the hotel and ended up walking around the city for three hours. We stayed in Germany (or was it Switzerland?) longer than planned, because my dad was suffering from a bad back and had to get regular shots for a period of time. As we continued our journey to London, we went off the beaten tracks, visiting castles on our way. I have very fond and wonderful memories of this trip.
>
> When we finally arrived in London, summer vacation had started for my sister and brothers. We rented a flat where we passed the days playing Risk and spending time together. I loved my siblings and they loved me. It was a wonderful summer with my whole family together.

In September, my parents announced that I would be staying on in England. I don't remember caring much about what I was doing. I did what I was told. It was not like today's children, with whom consensus must be achieved for every decision made for them! My dad drove back to Tehran with my grandmother, who also happened to be in Europe at the time. I remember this because my grandma was taking coffee back to Iran and they were stopped at the border on the suspicion that this was some form of drug! My father was mad at her saying, 'I told you not to bring anything with you!' After being harassed for a while they were finally released.

My mother stayed on in England with me and decided to go to hair design school at Vidal Sassoon. Before leaving, my father had promised that on her return to Iran, he would open a hair salon for her. This, of course, never happened since he had the foresight that she probably would not charge her friends and family, who would be her likely customers!

After our blissful summer holidays, one day I was taken to a boarding house. I was told that, going forward, I would be living at that house. The next day the lady of the house, Mrs Hyde, took me to the bus stop to show me my path to the bus stop and then to my new school, which was quite a long walk, a section of which was a path that went through a dark cemetery. That was it. From that day on, I made the journey on my own. I didn't know a word of English, but I survived. I later found out that Mrs Hyde's sister and brother-in-law were Titanic survivors! The Hydes were a lovely family and very kind to me though not really involved in my life. Other boarders were living there too, but since it wasn't a favourable time of my life, I never kept up my relationship with any of them.

I will never forget the first night I arrived at the Hydes'. The family asked my name. I said 'Saghi' and their reaction was, 'You have to change that name to Sally'. I believe that really impacted my life. I was no longer Saghi, but was now Sally. It changed my identity and personality for a period of time. I continued to be Sally for the next five years! Only once I left boarding school for Cannes, France, did I go back to being Saghi, finding my identity again.

Saghi, in Farsi, means the woman who pours the wine and has a very sensual connotation, an appropriate name for Saghi's free-spirited character.

My mother's beauty school lasted six months, during which time I boarded at the Hydes' so that I would start to get used to being a boarder. During the week, I went to school and visited my mother and brother on weekends. Once my mother returned to Iran, I continued to live in London at the Hydes'. My siblings were also all attending their own schools and I would get to see them on weekends.

While she was in London, my mother had purchased an apartment. This proved to be of great value to me in later years, which I will tell you about later! Surprisingly, my mother's departure wasn't that traumatic for me. I was very quiet and submissive and did not question my parents' decisions. What was more traumatizing than her departure was the day my mother took me to her salon to trim my hair. She put my hair into a ponytail and then cut it off! That is one of my most disturbing memories, even more than leaving my mother at an early age! I had accepted that they had my best interest at heart as they had done the same for my other siblings. I never felt they were abandoning me. But cutting my hair was truly horrible.

At the boarding house, there was another Persian girl, but we were absolutely forbidden to speak Farsi. So, in three months I learned English perfectly. At first I couldn't understand that people couldn't speak Farsi and thought that they weren't speaking Farsi just to get to me. But in three months, I spoke English fluently and, later, also learned to speak French fluently.

Once my siblings left London, I was sent to a boarding school. I was fourteen at the time. I spent the next two years at my new school. By this time, I had already been living in London for three years but boarding school was the worst time for me. I felt alone and alienated. Prior to this, I was living with a kind family and I had the weekends with my family to look forward to. Also, I had my best friend, Karen, the popular girl at my day school who, to me, was the most beautiful blue-eyed, blond-haired girl I had ever seen and was also kind and fun. She also taught me English. But now all I had to look forward to was the distant holidays when my mom would come to London, or I would meet her in Majorca or go to Iran.

The night before I left for boarding school, I begged my mother and brother to take me to see the movie *The Exorcist*, just out on the big screen. I loved scary movies, but this movie completely traumatized me. I began to have a phobia of the night and of being alone. The first year at school I lived with a lot of fear.

I went to Moira House School in Eastbourne. Just saying the name now is scary for me because I hated being there so much. The building I lived in was separate from the rest of the school. Even when going to the bathroom during the day, I was frightened of closing the door, or of returning to the dorm to change. I was afraid of being alone in this boarding school and had developed a terrible night phobia. It was the most depressing time of my life.

We were only allowed out of the school to go to town two hours per week. It was really hard for me at first, but soon I started to make good friends with two other Persian girls at my school. I felt many of the girls hated me; they were just horrible kids. We had nothing in common and trying to get along with the British characteristics was tough for me. At the time, the school was a very homogenous environment, mostly British girls. Eventually, I became friendly with the older English girls who were also known as the 'bad' girls. I could identify better with them since they were more worldly and adventurous.

At school, there was a hermaphrodite who became my friend. He was a genius and a pianist. I refer to him as 'he' although he was really a 'she' at our school. At first, he had gone to a boy's school and they were so horrible to him that his parents decided to switch him to an all-girls boarding school. He was such a sensitive, soft and gentle guy. He came to school as a sixth former so was allowed to wear his own clothes. I remember him always in pants and not in skirts as the other girls had to wear. Nevertheless, he was accepted by everyone at school the way he was.

In England, people didn't appear racist and we never thought about prejudice and race. I learned about racism only when I came to the U.S. and especially to Washington, DC. Here I became aware of discrimination in its different forms. Before this time there were no distinctions in my mind.

I didn't have a guardian but the school had assigned me to a holiday home. A few other girls and I would spend our one-week term break at that home. It was called Bateman's and the author Rudyard Kipling is known to have lived there for over thirty years. The house was also a museum, so visitors passed through during the day. It was a scary, old stone house and seemed miserable at the time. Now that I think back, it was quite a beautiful house. I was in a dormitory with six other girls. I remember I was so frightened to get up to go to the bathroom at night. It was so cold and pitch black.

But the grounds were beautiful. Thinking back, I can't believe I was actually living in Kipling's old house and I never even bothered to visit the museum! We didn't appreciate these things then. We were just trying to survive. Our interests were limited to things like the *Top of the Pops* on television every week, where we watched pop artists like Donny Osmond, who I was desperately in love with. Actually, when I was thirteen and living in London, I got myself invited to a garden party to meet him.

Saghi laughs and pauses to remember this episode! She is naturally a positive person and always so full of life. People are drawn to her warmth and uplifting energy.

> How did I manage to get myself into the garden party at this age? I wouldn't be surprised if I managed that today and wiggled myself into a party, but how did I do it then? That was the beginning of my 'wiggle'!
>
> Anyway, I became good friends with the older girls who were studying for their A-Levels. Although they were two years my senior, they had taken a liking to me. They considered me their source of fun. The British system was such that after completing O-Levels, two further years in the sixth form led to A-Levels, which was a requirement for admission to British universities. The first year was a prep year and the second the exam. Also, if the required number of O-Levels had not been passed in the fifth form, the girls had the option to stay on for the first year of sixth form to redo their O-Levels. I wouldn't be surprised if my friends were in the second redo category!
>
> That was the beginning of my partying! The sixth-form girls lived in the House across the street from the main school building referred to as

the Mansion. I was the only girl lower than the sixth form invited to the Mansion. I was not yet physically fully developed as a woman and had only just got my period, whereas the sixth-form girls were already developed as these voluptuous young ladies. However, I was a valuable asset as a friend!

The London apartment was at my disposal while my mother was back in Iran. My parents always had 100 per cent trust in me. So, if I said, at the age of fifteen, that I didn't want to go to the Kipling House for the breaks and wanted to go to the London apartment instead, they would agree! So, with my friends Kay and Sarah, we would go to *my* London apartment, which was in Maida Vale – a lovely area – and there we partied all the time. Kay, a gorgeous young lady who was the niece of a famous arms dealer and Esra, his daughter and Kay's cousin, also her age, would join us. I met many interesting, fun people through them and we partied. Through Kay, I got to meet the who's who of the Arab princes living in London. One time, Prince S came and picked me up in his Rolls Royce and asked where to take me for lunch. I said Wimpy's, like any kid my age would!

'There is a Tour d'Argent in Paris; let's go there', he said.

'No, I want to go to Wimpy's'.

'Saghi, I'm a prince, for god's sake!'

It was fun for me to have the Prince take me to Wimpy's and watch his face, but he was a trouper. He would sometimes take me to different garages where he had parked his fleet of cars to impress me, but I was not at all interested in him. It may have impressed me now, but not then, not in the least! I don't remember being a big drinker at the time, but I did like to party even then. My favourite memory of boarding school was that we could travel to London on the term breaks, but also get passes during the term on weekends to go up to London.

The school was very structured and disciplined. What I hated the most was the severe discipline. Every morning we lined up, had to shake hands and curtsy before the teacher who examined our fingernails and the length of our skirts. Then we went to the recreational room until it was time for the assembly of the whole school to sing hymns. I also hated the 10 a.m. break when the matron handed out our mail. Although I looked forward to that time of the day in the hope of receiving mail, I was often disappointed because I rarely did, except on occasion from my mother. I have kept every one of those letters. If it wasn't for my friends, I don't know what I would have done at that school.

I was a fourth former when I first arrived at school. Each year, we were assigned to create a theme-based fun dinner for the whole school to attend. The girls worked on this project for months to really transform the entire room and make appropriate costumes. I was very impressed by this major accomplishment. We also had a few Shakespeare plays like *The Tempest*, where we created all the costumes and décor ourselves.

Saghi continues to enjoy costume parties and does a lot of preparations for her annual Halloween party at her house.

> During the time I was at school, our headmistress changed to a headmaster, Mr Underwood. I have no recollection of any other teacher or any of my classes. I hated it so much that I have erased memory of all of them, or even which O-Level subjects I took at school.
>
> I don't really have specific bad memories, just bad feelings around my experience. It is in my character to make the best of everything. So, I have kept the good memories and let go of the bad ones.
>
> For two hours on Sundays, we were allowed to go to Eastbourne. Our school was on a hill and going to town was easy. We just ran down the hill as fast as we could, away from that ridiculous place. Coming back was not so easy! Our favourite pastime in town was to go to the supermarket and buy a jar of mixed spicy pickles, sit on the bench and eat them. That was the most exciting part of our outing.
>
> At school, we had many duties, one of which was dishwashing and kitchen duties. To this day, I can recall the horrible smell of the dishwasher. Our food was average and we were forced to eat everything. That taught me not to be fussy about food such as Brussel sprouts, which I hated then but love now.
>
> What was really important to me were my friends and the fun we had like enjoying the pickles. I looked forward to our outing each week. Episodic events, such as assembly, when we sang the hymn 'Morning Has Broken', have also stayed with me! I had a terrible voice and it was hard for me to sing, even with the entire school singing. Those are the things that I recall. I can't even picture what our classrooms looked like.
>
> I have searched for some of my old friends and found two of them on Facebook. One is my Facebook friend, Mariam, whom I keep in touch with now. We were close friends in school, both feeling alienated as foreigners. She was more like my sister then. The other was Haleh, who is living in Florida, but with whom I am not in contact. We were very different from each other and were not that close at school. I also stayed in contact with my family through letters, phone calls and sometimes visiting them during the holidays.
>
> I can't remember how the holiday travel arrangements were made. I do remember that in her letters, my mother would send me money and a shopping list of items I was to purchase for her and her friends, from underwear to outer clothing, before returning to Iran for the summer holidays. I can't imagine handing that kind of responsibility to a young fourteen-year-old; to go shopping, pack and get on a plane to go home. I can't see myself being so responsible at that early age, but I guess I must have been. When my mom came to London, all we would do was shop. She was a shopaholic! I would cry not to go and she would bribe me with a Wimpy. I loved the ketchup at

Wimpy's. We would start at the beginning of Marble Arch and walk through Oxford Street, down to Bond Street and then through all the side roads. We would go down one side and come up the other, leaving some packages in the stores, catching a cab to take us home at the end of the day, recouping all the packages on the way.

At one point my mom had a boutique in Iran, since my Dad was always trying to keep her busy. Most of her clients were her friends and family so she wouldn't charge them for their purchases and then the friends of these friends would also come and the Persian *taarof*[3] would start, so she never made any money from her boutique. That's why he never opened the hair salon either. When she finished the hair stylist school, he said to her: 'Are you crazy? Did you really think I would open a salon for you after the boutique experience? Just do your friends' and family's hair without opening up a salon. I've already invested in six month of schooling'. She held a grudge about this forever.

What I have taken away from the experience of boarding school is that I learned not to be shy and became independent. It taught me how to be alone and enjoy my own company, how to get things done for myself and make the most of any situation I may be in. I always manage to have a good laugh with myself! I think I was much less spoilt as a result and less high maintenance. I also developed a sense of responsibility, but the experience affected me in that I don't do well with authority, to being told what to do. When later in life I got into modelling, I hated it because I didn't like to be judged by whether my fingernails were done or not! I never paid much attention to my nails until just lately!

I didn't always have very high self-esteem. I was very small in height for a long time and painfully shy. I grew taller later than normal, suddenly growing fast and painfully before my period, to my present five-foot-nine-inch height. I don't remember being very confident either. I didn't have many friends at my school in Iran. The one friend I did have, though, continues to be my friend. And since then all the friends I have made remain in my life to this day.

I was never under pressure by my family to perform well at school. Nobody really cared. My family didn't put many restrictions on us. We never had a bedtime; I'd usually pass out on the couch every night. I didn't have a disciplined life and although my father would tell me I was the brightest, the best and the light of his eyes, I was very passive as a child. If there were any arguments, he always took my word rather than my other siblings. He trusted my opinion more than the others. I had all the love that parents can possibly give to their child. I don't know why I wasn't a happy, bubbly child. Or was I?

Although I was shy, I was naughty and enjoyed having the bad girls as my friends. My naughtiness was somewhat suppressed out of respect for my parents and my cultural upbringing. For example, when I was a young girl my parents never said to me not to have sex at a young age as we tell our kids. But it was instilled in me, without spoken words, that I wasn't to have sex until I got married. It was expected of me because of my Iranian culture; we were just brought up that way. When I was eleven, one of my girlfriends told me how she had had sex at the bus stop. I was amazed and intrigued but knew that I would never be doing that.

There was a feeling of independence from being sent away, but I never felt abandoned. I'm not so open with my emotions, but my body reacts and things show up physically for me. For example, my mom passed away when I was eighteen and I went from a size zero to a size twelve. When my father then passed away five years ago it marked the beginning of my severe allergies. My emotions manifest as negative physical reactions.

I never felt guilt for being sent away or that I had to appreciate what had been done for me. My parents never pushed or pressured me into doing anything specific or for high performance at school. It wasn't their priority at all. They just wanted me to have some sort of education and come home. My dad always told me that I didn't need to go to university. 'I sent your siblings and what good did it do them?' He said to me that after school I would be continuing my studies at a finishing school and that would be that, with the plan being that after my studies I would return to Iran and work with my father. We were wealthy and my future was set. Or so we thought. That never actually happened since by that time the revolution was in full force and everyone was just trying to survive.

Saghi's parents remained in Iran after the revolution, but she never went back to live there after her schooling. She continued to remain in France and then went to California, where some of her extended family lived post-revolution.

The turning point in my life was this. I was in Iran during the summer holidays. It was three weeks before I was to go back to Moira House and that day we had company at home. I was sitting behind the couch in the living room and crying, in anticipation of my return to school. My father found me and asked:

> 'Saghi joon,[4] what's wrong? Why are you crying?'
> 'Dad, I'm sorry'.
> 'Go wash your face and come to my office in five minutes'.

I straightened myself out before going to see him, scared that he would tell me off for embarrassing him in front of his guests. Instead he repeated his question:

> 'Why are you crying?'
> 'I hate my school and I don't want to go back'.
> 'I'm so, so sorry. I thought after two years you would get used to it. Wipe your tears. You will never have to go back there again'.

That was the end of that. So instead of being shipped to England with my skirt, cloak and the rest of my uniform, I was sent to the south of France. When I arrived at the airport in Cannes, my gay headmaster picked me up from the airport in his convertible Spider. With the wind blowing in my hair and the Cote d'Azur sun warming my face, I thought to myself, 'What is happening to me …?' and from that moment I blossomed. I lost 'Sally' and was 'Saghi' again! I knew that this is where I belonged.

That was the beginning of the three most beautiful years of my life. I was not in the depressing Moira House anymore; I was in sunny Cannes and free as a bird! What more would anyone want? This is why most of my memories of Moira House have been erased. I hated it so much: I put it out of my head and never thought about those years again.

Saghi lights up as she starts the story of her years in France. The dark cloud that seemed to cover her during our talk about boarding school suddenly lifts, as with a big smile, she relives being in the sports car with her hair flowing in the wind!

In France, I stayed with a family. From the first day, they put a key in my hand and said:

'Don't ask us what to do, you're on your own. Breakfast is at this time, lunch at this time and dinner at this time. Don't expect us to check your homework or ask if you can watch television, or if you can go out'.

I was in shock! Imagine being in Cannes, the best town in the world, in a beautiful house, beautiful room and fun, beautiful people. I didn't speak with the family for three years. My French wasn't that great at the beginning of my stay, and they didn't speak English. The man of the house was really weird. One day he came into the room and closed the door and asked me to kiss him. I shouted, 'If you don't get out of my room I will scream'. I knew exactly what he was looking for. I was strong, not the weak, shy little Sally anymore. I was back to being Saghi!

I had finished my O-Levels in my boarding school in fifth form. In Cannes, I went to school to learn French. I didn't like the French school since everyone in my class spoke English and my French didn't improve one bit. It felt like a waste of time. So, I went to the American section of the Chateaubriand School to complete my eleventh and twelfth grade.

Today, Saghi is married and has a sixteen-year-old son. She is a stay-at-home mum, enjoying her days with her family and friends. Since this interview, Saghi was inspired to find and reconnect with many of her Moira House school friends and has visited one of them on her travels through Italy last summer.

Notes

1   Paykan Javanan was an Iranian produced car, based on the British Hillman, popular in Iran between the 1960s and 1990s and a source of pride for the Iranian manufacturers.

The government of the Shah Mohammad Reza Pahlavi had promised that one day every Iranian would own a Paykan.
2   Passing under the Quran is an Iranian tradition for travellers. A bowl of water, a Quran and a mirror are placed on a tray and each traveller passes under the tray three times. Once the last traveller has completed the passage, the water is thrown behind their path, wishing them a safe journey.
3   *Taarof* is a unique and charming cultural practice that is designed to show civility and respect for others specially to those in higher social class, elderly and strangers.
4   *Joon*, literally meaning 'life', is a Persian term of endearment and respect often used among friends with the version of *Jaan* used for older and more distant relations and associates.

5
LETTERS OF HOPE

Dory's story

Charters Towers School, Bexhill-on-Sea, Sussex (1976–1977)
Lowther College, Bodelwyddan, North Wales (1977–1979)

Roya met Dory in Silver Spring, Maryland, at a coach training weekend. As the only Persians in a small group of people, their connection was immediate. They subsequently remained in touch and shared their coaching experiences. When Roya told Dory about her impending book, Dory revealed that she and her sisters had also been sent to boarding school in England and, coincidentally, for a short time had been at Roya's school.

> I was shipped to boarding school in 1976 with my two younger sisters. In my family, we are six sisters and one brother! My two older sisters were already married. My third sister went to boarding school the year before us and stayed only for one year. When we left Iran, I was fifteen and my younger sisters were thirteen and eleven. First, we were sent to Charters Towers School in Bexhill-on-Sea and later to Lowther College in North Wales.
>
> On our first trip to England we were accompanied by my parents. They had a flat in London and were already spending considerable time there. Following this trip and their return to Iran, my uncle, a resident of the U.K., became our guardian. Although his role was not very significant, he was responsible for us during the periods my parents were not in England. He picked us up from the airport and dropped us off at the train station to go to school. During the years that we were at school, only once did we go back to Iran for a holiday. Instead, my parents would come to London and stay in the city.
>
> The decision to send us to England was a total surprise to all three of us since we were not consulted. My parents knew a family friend whose daughter had gone to boarding school and, without doing any research or finding out how we would feel about it, we were sent off. It was the 'in-thing' to do. None of us spoke much English. The extent of my English was if someone stepped on my foot I would say 'thank you'. When I arrived at Charters Towers, I was placed in a dorm with four other girls. It was terrible. I had been taken away from the only environment I knew without any consultation. That's what was so traumatizing.
>
> My family was not at all religious. But out of desperation, I took on *Namaz*, the Muslim prayer. I remember one time I was praying on my bed. There was not much space in our dorm of four. I had placed a *chador*[1] (actually it was a bed sheet) over my head. One of my roommates walked in and started screaming thinking she had seen a ghost!

Many of us took up prayer to console ourselves, not because of any strong religious belief. Most of us had never prayed before and although we had learned to recite the Muslim *Namaz* in Arabic, had no idea what the words meant. Much like Fereshteh (Chapter 2), who was able to console herself in the church with tears, Dory and others found relief in faith, giving them hope.

> Then I discovered Bob Dylan. He saved me. My roommate played his music and although I didn't understand the words, I would cry and cry. I cried

so much that year. Our school permitted us to call home from the office. I used my weekly allowance to call but it happened so often that my parents directed the school not to let me call anymore. My last call to my mother is vivid in my memory because I said to her: 'I hate you, I hope you all suffer for sending us here'.

My sister Marjaneh had a traumatizing experience that first year. In the middle of the night she woke up to see her roommates having oral sex. She had never heard of or seen homosexual behaviour. Watching these girls having sex at the age of eleven shocked and troubled her deeply. She later told me that she woke shaking and crying. We were only allowed to be with each other as sisters during Sunday prayers so I wasn't able to console her through that disturbing experience. Naturally, being the oldest of three, I felt responsible for my two younger sisters.

I remember our first trip alone on the train to school. It was raining and we arrived at the station at night with our big suitcases. As we waited for someone to pick us up, my sisters began to cry. I felt devastated myself, but tried to be the brave one consoling them. I was only sixteen.

Before I arrived, there was another Persian girl who had been in the school for several years. She was pivotal in my adjustment. She encouraged me to believe that things would get better. It was so difficult not knowing the English language. I had classes in chemistry and physics. Each page would literally take me hours to understand. Fortunately, Mr Foster, my science teacher at Charters Towers, was a very kind and patient man.

While at Charters Towers, I wrote letters to every person I knew. The purpose being to receive letters back. Once I received so many letters that it was brought to me on a big tray. All the girls were jealous. I would keep these letters, read them one at a time and savour each one. It saddened me to read about the fun my friends were having at school in Iran without me. That is when I began my habit of writing a diary, which I continue today. I have kept my diaries from my days at Charters Towers.

Marjaneh, my sister, ran away twice. She would just leave the school and the police would find her and bring her back. When my parents learned about this, they realized that we really were unhappy. So, they removed us from Charters Towers and placed us in another school, this time in Lowther College, North Wales. There were two other Persian girls at this school, Golnaz and Azita. I became good friends with the foreign girls, but not so much with the British.

This new school looked like Hogwarts[2] in the Harry Potter books. Originally, it was a castle, which in later years was turned into a museum and an art centre. Part of the castle is now used as a hotel, called Bodelwyddan Castle[3] and is what you imagine an old castle to be. Here, I was completely isolated from my sisters. Eating was my only consolation so I got really fat. Many of my memories of boarding school have been completely repressed because I hated it so much. Although I hated Charters Towers, I had become familiar with it. Moving to another school, it was hard to readjust again. The new school was even further away from London. At least when I was in Charters Towers, I was close enough to visit my parents when they were in London.

One day, I was sitting under a tree where I made a pact with myself: 'Whatever happens you will survive'. My survival method was that I became the class clown, making people laugh. It is difficult to remember those days except for the sadness in my heart, my emotions and feelings. My memories of walks by the sea are of the dismal fog, dampness and the seagulls flying overhead. Nothing else!

All my sisters and I ever did was complain. So, after being at the school in Wales for a year and a half, my parents decided to move my sisters to an American day school in London. By this time I had finished my O- and A-Levels and was to leave for the U.S. to begin my university studies. The Iranian Revolution was now underway and my parents had moved permanently to London. My father was retired, so he and my mother took turns going back and forth to Iran to take care of their commitments back home.

I felt huge anger towards my parents for a long time. I went through many years of therapy including Eye Movement Desensitization and Reprocessing, normally used for trauma patients. When the therapist asked me about the traumatizing experiences of my life, I said to him, 'I haven't had any traumatic experience'. To me trauma was physical abuse, but the therapist educated me that trauma doesn't have to be physical abuse; that even a word that someone says to you can negatively affect you. It's the interpretation of that event that can be traumatic. All of a sudden, my memories took me back to Lowther College, in the piano room in that old castle, feeling so alone. Through therapy, I recognized all the anger I had built up towards my parents. I realized that those years had killed a very important part of me – my playful side. I used to be an extremely popular kid in Iran, a top student in my class with lots of friends, including a boyfriend. I was like a flower blooming and then during the most important years of my life – my adolescence – that flower stopped blooming. I felt I had been deprived of that time. Basically, the message I had taken from my parents was that I had no control over my life. I had not chosen to go away to school, I was just packed off and sent away.

As a Persian girl, I was brought up to be submissive. I never questioned my parents' actions until I started living in the West and going to therapy. Then my eyes were opened to the trauma I had endured. I realized that the world is a harsh place and it is up to me to protect myself. I blamed my parents and resented them, although on the surface I would never show them my true feelings. I still begrudge them a little. The difference is that now my sisters and I openly tell my mother how much we were hurt.

I can understand sending children to boarding school if one comes from a broken family and if parents are trying to save their children from the unrest at home. But we had a happy home; there was no reason to send us away. I don't think much thought had gone into their decision to send us off. My parents were just following what was fashionable in the families of the elite in Iran. It was never a question of feeling unloved by my parents. I always felt loved by them. That's why it was such a shock to me. I kept wondering: What happened? What did I do wrong to be punished this way?

I now know that many of my personal characteristics were developed because I had to survive boarding school. I am an easy going, malleable person. Partly due to my early limitations in language, I developed an aptitude for reading people, with few verbal cues and ascertaining their feelings. I believe I am also more compassionate than most. I empathize with and want to help the downtrodden. I used to be considered the black sheep in my family because I loved my friends and enjoyed hanging out with them. To this day, my family believes that I prefer to spend more time with my friends than with them, although that is not true. I think my boarding school experience made me become somewhat of an introvert. I like my time alone and am very independent. It's just a different kind of love. Even when I was in Iran, I never wanted to come home. I was just so social. I needed the interaction of a group.

My therapist summarized my boarding school experience as follows: 'This blooming flower was plucked from the garden and planted in a desert of salt water. How did you expect it to bloom? You just did what you could and have bloomed into something you are now'.

Having been brought up in the stoic English culture, it was difficult for me at that time to show emotion. I believed showing emotion was a sign of weakness. It was silly and I was very judgmental about it. Now, with the work I've been doing on myself and the coach training, it's all coming back and cracking open. People open up to their vulnerabilities in different ways and at different periods of their lives.

My source of support came from reading books and writing in my journal. I don't know any different life than the one I have had and I also don't know if I would have preferred a life in Iran without the boarding school experience. But I do wish I had had a different perspective while I was there and that I had taken advantage of all that was available to me at the time. I might have even enjoyed it!

Once I hosted a young boy from England at my home in Washington DC for a month. He too had gone to boarding school. He helped me in understanding the experience from his perspective. When I asked him if he enjoyed being at boarding school, he replied, 'What is wrong with living in a place with kids your own age, where you are learning, having fun and then going home on weekends?' Of course, the difference was that in his situation, he got to go home on weekends!

As I reflect on my past, I realize that I always want to be busy. Part of this need for busyness is a way to protect myself against focusing on the pain I have carried with me and with the idea of just 'being'. I have been working on self-improvement for many years with meditation and counselling and now find I'm increasingly more at ease with being present.

The highlight of being a boarder was the exposure to different cultures and the connections I made. This is important to me to this day. My best friend from school was a girl called Malak from Saudi Arabia. At the end of the school year, we would each have an autograph book where friends would reflect on the relationship they had with each other. It was a reinforcement of what we had experienced together and an acknowledgement of the people we had become. I had always been told that I was funny. In therapy, I discovered that when I was recounting something personally hurtful, I would laugh, although I would be doing this unconsciously. I learned then that by laughing you can ease the pain of your experience. Underneath the laughter, I was covering something else that was going on. I have kept these autograph books.

I have good memories of school dances. In Wales the nearby boys' school bused their students to our school. I remember being excited about seeing these ugly, pimply things! Following the dance, we sometimes took the train to London to meet these boys again.

Occasionally, we would raid the tuck shop and the kitchen. One night, we jumped over the wall of the castle to sneak into town. I got so fat during that period that I couldn't fit into my pants anymore. I had to make two holes on either side and pull a string between the two sides so I wouldn't lose them. In Wales, they would bring big bottles of cold milk, which were delicious. And the sheep in Wales were different from any sheep I had ever seen. I remember being in the meadows, seeing the sheep and thinking how lucky they are that they don't have to go to class.

At Christmas, the school catered turkey and plum pudding. The chef would come out and we would cheer him with 'Hip, Hip Hurray' for the turkey. A girl who shared a room with me got pregnant by the chef's son. He impregnated another girl too! Both girls had to leave school. This was quite a memorable event at school.

The end of the year play also brings back good memories. I still remember and feel nostalgic today when I hear the songs we sang at assembly. I took piano, cooking and needlework classes. I learned how to type. I was so bored that sometimes I would just practice typing my book.

I believe that by being at boarding school many of my personal characteristics were suppressed, which may have had a chance to develop otherwise. I became fearful and, as a result, contained my feelings. From an early age, I was made to believe my voice didn't count and that I shouldn't make a 'splash'. As a result, I reacted by sabotaging rules and jumping over fences. But, I was never a leader. With my friends, we were just together, one unit. If I had any leadership potential I think boarding school suppressed that. I'm not afraid to try new things, although I am afraid to show my vulnerabilities.

But now I see that within my family all the things I have done, I have initiated and taken the risk for, without consulting with others. I'm responsible and capable. My word means something. I lead my own life and like to carve it out the way I want it to be.

I'm hoping to take coaching to Iran since therapy, arguably, has a stigma attached to it. Coaching could be more acceptable. I want to do some video workshops to reach a greater population as well as provide coaching for the girls in the Omid Foundation,[4] which my younger sister Marjaneh established and I have been involved in for years. I think the impetus or genesis of Omid for my sister is also a result of the suffering she experienced. She empathizes with people who are discarded, displaced or disconnected from society.

Marjaneh, who completed her graduate studies in social psychology at the London School of Economics and the University of Cambridge, focuses her work with the Omid Foundation on supporting women who suffer domestic violence. She lives in London with her husband but spends half her time in Iran at her foundation, while the other half she spends travelling raising the much-needed funds. Under her leadership, the foundation has thrived. She does not have children of her own and considers these girls to be her children.

Dory now lives in Bethesda, Maryland, with her husband and daughter who is presently in college. Dory continues her coaching practice, focusing her work on youth.

Notes

1. A chador is a full-body-length semicircle of fabric (often black) open in the front and tossed over the woman's head. It is held closed under the chin with one hand and partly tucked under one arm. Devout women wear a chador for the Muslim prayer and/or while in the presence of men. After the revolution, it became a requirement for all women in Iran to cover themselves in public.
2. The Hogwarts School of Witchcraft and Wizardry is a fictional British school of magic, made popular by the Harry Potter novels.
3. Bodelwyddan Castle, a manor house in Wales, built around 1460 by the Humphreys family, had many reports of ghost sightings.
4. The OMID Foundation is an organization that supports Iranian and Afghan women, who are victims of sexual, physical or mental abuse, by providing them with educational and vocational training. The goal of the organization is to transform lives by making each girl financially and socially independent.

6
THE REBEL WITHIN

Shirley's story
Charters Towers School, Bexhill-on-Sea, Sussex (1964–1969)

68 A life lived

From the age of twelve, Shirley was a force to be reckoned with. She was taller than her friend Roya (Chapter 1) and, unlike her, she had a loud, commanding voice. She has a powerful presence and a charisma that has not changed throughout the years. She speaks her mind when others might censor their opinions to be politically correct! She has a vast conglomeration of friends spread across the globe and, therefore, is always surrounded by people wherever she goes. Roya speaks of Shirley as a loyal, loving friend who can always be depended on.

I was trouble. I couldn't wait to get out of Iran.

My brother was in Carmel College[1] outside London and the headmaster had come to visit Iran a few years back. The school was just starting to become co-ed, so I told my father I wanted to go there too. My father was not happy about the idea of girls and boys living under the same roof. As a compromise, since my older sister Flora was living in London at the time, I was permitted to go and be with her. She would become my guardian and find me an appropriate school. Flora found Charters Towers School through a friend whose daughter was already at the school and was about to finish her studies.

At the time, I was in the sixth grade at the Etefagh School[2] in Tehran. My father used his connections to get me accepted late in the summer. Since I was the youngest of four children and the last child at home, my mother didn't want me to leave. She kept checking with me: 'Are you sure you want to go? If you go you won't be here anymore!' But I just couldn't wait to leave: 'Yes, I'm going'.

Flora, who had been living in London, had come back to Iran, got married and had two sons. She was now back living in London with her family. Her oldest son, Michael, is only three years younger than me and Stevie, her second son, three years younger than Michael. So, it was a very easy transition for me. I went off to the familiarity of my sister's household, to be with my nephews, who were like brothers to me.

When I first arrived, Flora took me to Dickins & Jones to buy my uniform and Zahra, her maid, sewed all the name labels on to my new clothes. I was so excited about my new brown and gold uniform. I was ready to take off on my own personal adventure. During that same period, my cousin Jaleh was sent to another boarding school in a different town.

My sister and her husband packed Jaleh and me into their car and drove us to our respective schools. We arrived at House I in Charters Towers where Matron Sharpus, in her crisp white uniform, greeted us. She led us up a flight of stairs to the first dorm on the right. This was a two-person dorm. My roommate was a girl from Africa by the name of Sue. I had no problem with her being black since I was colour blind to race. As Flora and her husband came in to bring my luggage, Flora was shocked and upset that I was placed in a room with a black girl. She kept asking me, 'Are you OK here?' I was absolutely fine. There was no difference for me – but Flora was not fine! She had been sent to boarding school in the U.S. at the age of eight in the early 1950s, during the peak of segregation, and that had impacted her.

Although apprehensive about my dorm situation, my family finally left me but must have called the school ten times that day to speak to me! Finally, the next day my sister could not stand it any longer; she called the headmistress, Ms McGarry, and told her: 'I want you to move Shirley from that room. I don't want her to be in a room with a black girl'. I don't know what she was thinking. Perhaps because of her experience in the U.S., her understanding (or lack thereof) of segregation and the fear that she had developed living in the U.S., she thought the colour might rub off on me! I still don't understand her shocking reasoning at the time. Anyway, Miss McGarry called me into her office and asked if I was alright in my room, to which I replied 'yes'. But being a child who always looked for trouble, I wanted to be in a room with more people and so I said that I preferred to be moved. I didn't know anything about the 'colour' situation until the Christmas holidays when Flora proudly announced how she had insisted to have my room changed. That is when I realized why Miss McGarry was so hard on me. She assumed that I, like my sister, was prejudiced.

I was finally moved to a room next to the matron's room, Fra Angelico, where there were seven other girls, Sylvia, Diana, a few others – and Roya. I was happy.

My parents had sent us all to boarding school abroad from an early age. Perhaps being Jewish, they believed the schools were more integrated and provided us with a higher level of education. Flora was sent to the U.S. under the guardianship of my uncle John who lived in New York and had five daughters of his own. She would board during the week and spend the weekends at uncle John's. My sister Pari had also gone to boarding school in the U.S. and my brother was in the U.K.

It was nice to have my older sister as a guardian. Some weekends she would come to school and take my friends and me out on *exeats*. Each time I would tell her I would be bringing so-and-so with me. From that early time, I always had my 'entourage'!

Shirley has kept her friends from all walks of life. To this day, she is never without her 'entourage', wherever she goes.

I didn't know English when I first arrived, only what I had learned at school in Iran. The first term, I hardly spoke and took it all in. When I came back to school from Christmas holidays, it became like a verbal diarrhoea for me. No one could stop me anymore! I thought if I spoke louder they would understand me better. Every term the report from Miss McGarry was 'Shirley must learn how to whisper!'

I was always in trouble. A hedge separated our school from the boys' school next door. The second year when I was in House II, a group of girls arranged with the boys in the neighbouring school to come to our dorm, by way of the fire escape ladder. There were about six of us in that dorm. The boys were to throw a stone at our window to notify us so we would lower the ladder. I was sleeping by the window so after the silence bell I was to let down the ladder. The boys crawled across my bed with their dirty shoes, as they entered our room. There were three boys, but I was not involved with any of them; I was just the 'ladder girl'. It was more the English girls who were connecting with the boys, giggling and doing whatever they were doing. I was just observing! They giggled and were so noisy that eventually the matron heard, walked in, turned on the lights and saw these boys in our room. In shock, she ushered the boys out the front door. We were in serious trouble after that and had to go to Miss McGarry's office the next day. One by one we went in and were interrogated. I told her that I was only the ladder girl. She questioned me in detail:

'Did any of the boys sit on your bed?'
'No, Miss McGarry'.
'Did they touch you?'
'No, Miss McGarry'.

As I said, I had been an observer. Later, the other girls told me that the interrogation was more detailed as to where they had been touched, which part of their body and some other very embarrassing questions. I guess she was responsible for us and had to know the extent of this raid!

It hadn't taken long. I had already been on Miss McGarry's blacklist from day one with the Sue episode. Her perception of me was of a racist. That was of course false. I didn't know anything about prejudice. I had never seen anyone different from myself before, except I knew that compared to Silvia, a very light-skinned blond girl in our dorm, I was dark! As far as I was concerned, I was one of the many girls with a darker skin colour. Our school had a strong multi-racial culture and any prejudice was frowned upon.

By now, I had made up for the first term when I had been quiet. Now I was always getting into trouble because I was plain naughty. Once I put mustard on the matron's chair in the dining room. After saying grace, we all sat down and the matron sat on the mustard laden chair. The back of her white uniform was all mustardy yellow like she had had diarrhoea. Again, I was sent to Miss McGarry's office. By this time, I was speaking English well but I didn't know all the expressions. Miss McGarry accused me of being a bad influence on the other girls. With her deep British accent and slow way of talking she said:

'Shirley ... (using my last name), pull your socks up'.

So, I bent over and pulled my socks up, not understanding that this was a metaphor for behaving properly! This was the first time I actually saw her smile, bemused by my reaction.

Other tricks we would play included putting a glass of water over the doors so that when someone opened the door the water would fall and soak them! Another time we had a school dance party in the assembly room. There were balloons all over so I grabbed one and was fiddling around with it. I used to bite my nails, so I started twirling this string around my tongue and managed to tie a knot around it. As I pulled it to loosen the knot, it became tighter around my tongue and got caught on one of my taste buds. I kept pulling to get it off. The more I pulled, the more the taste bud got swollen and the rubber kept getting tighter. The taste bud was bubbling over the knot. I couldn't get it off and I went to the nurse with the balloon tied to my mouth. The nurse didn't want to touch it so she called the doctor who cut it off with the surgical scissors. I had this swollen tongue for a few days!

Midnight feasts were always fun. I always brought back to school a stash of money. Our allowance was only about five shillings per week (equivalent to £6 sterling) or 10 shillings (equivalent to £12 sterling) if we were going on an *exeat*. So, my stash of money would serve to buy all the goodies for the feasts.

On Sundays, when the Christian girls went to church, the non-Christian girls would meet the girls of the same nationality and religion, to have a self-made religious period. Since I was the only Iranian Jewish girl at school, I joined other Jewish girls who were predominantly British. We never did anything religious in the group, just hung out. When I was older, I joined the rest of my Persian friends (the Muslim Iranians) and hung out with them, since they didn't do anything religious either.

Also, every Sunday we had a letter-writing period where we were forced to write to our families. I still remember the pre-stamped blue letters, which would have a three-way fold into its own envelope. When we had too much to say, we would write along the borders, hardly legible to anyone. At times when I didn't have much to say, I would write bigger to fill up the page! After lunch, we would rush to our respective common rooms to receive any letters and packages sent to us that day. My parents would write regularly so I was always waiting for these letters and the 'tuck' parcels (care packages) from Flora. She would send me sweets, food and sometimes clothes, on a regular basis.

Apart from my Persian friends, my other friends included two Portuguese girls, Theresa and Louise, who were also naughty. There was also Anthea. I also remember Diana whose mother died during the first year. She was in our class and had a crush on me. She would send me notes and tuck from the tuck shop. This was unusual since the crushes were usually directed at older girls by younger girls. I guess it was because I was a leader within the school!

I was never homesick; too busy making trouble. Along with Azy, my collaborator in mischief, our whole intention was to get into trouble. We were so spoilt in Iran that we thought this was just a game, testing how far we could push the envelope to see what we could get away with. The more trouble we got into, the more fun we had. We never took boarding school seriously because we knew our parents would always back us up. Azy and I looked at this whole experience as staged; it was a game. Our real life was back home. This was all for the education, the friendship and the bonding; beyond that it was not serious. Even to the extent of the O-Level exams, I didn't care a bit about studying. If I got six O-Levels or nine, at the end of the day I was going to get married and probably wouldn't be working. Our parents were not there to push us, or at least mine weren't.

I spent Christmas holidays with my nephews and we would go skiing. Easter holidays I would go to Iran and in the summers my parents would come to London and we would go to the south of France for part of the time and then to Iran.

When I was fourteen, I went to Iran for my cousin Mahnaz's wedding, which was an extremely glamorous wedding and written up by *Zan-e-Rooz*.[3] The dresses worn by my sister and I were even highlighted in the article. It was a big shebang at one of the big hotels of the time, Hilton or Sheraton or something. At the wedding, there was this guy with green eyes who fancied me. Although I was only fourteen, after the wedding we arranged to meet and I would sneak out in the afternoons and meet him. When I went back to school we continued to communicate and he would send me letters and teddies. He was about twenty-one. Miss McGarry became aware of these and intercepted his letters to me. She sent a pile of these letters to Flora. Flora in turn told my father, which got me into trouble. This kind of behaviour was not acceptable and was frowned upon, although we hadn't done anything except to kiss.

The young man was very persistent, but my family knew his reputation and did not trust him. He was interested in catching one of the girls from my family. Apparently, he had also tried with some of uncle John's girls. I didn't know his history. I was mesmerized by his beautiful green eyes. I always had a soft spot for green eyes! This all came to a head during the Christmas holidays, which was a very disturbing period for me. I was very upset at Flora for invading my privacy.

Shirley is the daughter of one of the most prominent and well-known industrialists in Iran. The unmarried daughters of the renowned people in Iran were sought after by many of the bachelors. They were looking to land a good marriage that would give them connections, opportunities and money. Because of this, many of the well-known families would marry within their own extended families, as Shirley eventually did. Shirley has a daughter from this marriage who she named after her friend Roya. The marriage, however, ended shortly after the revolution.

The biggest impact the school had on me was connecting with the girls who have become my lifelong friends, especially the small group of four Persian girls in our class. That was fantastic and cannot be replaced. Not only were we friends at school, but we were together during our holidays in Iran. Our close friendship continues to this day.

The other important influence was my exposure to art. I followed my passion for art and went to art school after my O-Levels. When I heard the names of the painters that we had been exposed to through our dorms,

I realized how educational and influential that had been for me. At Charters Towers each House had a focus on a period in art and each dorm was named after an artist from that period. It was a very cultured atmosphere. My handwriting is also good because of the emphasis on handwriting at the school. I look at my kids who can hardly write their names legibly. Also, manners and discipline were emphasized, such as how to eat and put our knife and fork down when we chew, or put them together when we are done eating, or sit up with our back straight and not put elbows on the table.

The first term I was there, I took two pieces of bread and put it on my plate. I loved breakfasts. The matron told me to take the bread one at a time. I had to cut it into half and then into quarters before spreading butter. It was very important to learn all of that. Also, things like how to make a bed with the hospital corners tucked in the sides, to respect the elders and to open the door for them. To this day, I feel uncomfortable not opening a door for my elders. I see these young, educated girls who have no table manners – never placing their cutlery together – and it really bothers me. When I see a crooked painting on the wall I have a need to straighten it! Little things like that which are now in my blood!

The team spirit and the competitiveness of the Houses to which we were assigned were wonderful. I loved all that, especially because I was good at sports and I was captain of this and that. I would never miss any practice even if I were sick. I just loved it.

All in all, I think it was an excellent experience for me. Because of my circumstances and the life I had in Iran, I could have turned out to be very spoilt. My father wasn't particularly strict, although he would discipline me with logic. He would talk to me about boys and who I should be looking for in marriage, even when I was as young as sixteen. He would tell me not to be around boys who were too young. Having these words in my ears, I was pressured into getting married as quickly as possible and so married my cousin (Jaleh's brother) at the age of eighteen.

Boarding school was liberating for me, from the strictness of all the dos and don'ts and whom I should or shouldn't be around. I could make my own decisions there and get into trouble without anyone watching over me and telling me what to do. As long as my parents knew we were safe, it was OK. I would say sorry and that was it. I was more monitored in Iran than in England, where I had my own little life.

I didn't want people to get a sense of the wealth of my family and what kind of power we had in Iran. I felt if they knew the truth, I would be rejected. I was always trying to play that down and didn't want to talk about it. I wanted to fit in. Because of that, perhaps, I would get into more trouble and create more havoc to distract from myself as a form of self-protection.

I would not send my children to boarding school unless they wanted to go themselves. In our time, it was the *shishi* – thing to do. Anyone who could, would send his or her kids to boarding school. When I was at school, I realized that we were the lucky ones because we had money. A lot of the other

> girls were there because they were from broken homes and the purpose was to kind of get rid of them. For us, it was more to go and have fun. Like sending kids off on holiday! Unlike others, I had a great support system with my friends and my sister nearby, although she was more like a guardian and was strict with me. After being with her for the holidays, I loved going back to school and the train rides.
>
> My only regret is that I didn't apply myself. I was capable of a lot but my parents never pushed me, which goes back to my background, the wealth we had and the society we lived in. It was just fine for me to get married, which is what I did. I married at an early age because I could do anything I wanted. We fell in love and that was it. There was no thought given to anything else. It could have been any guy I would have fallen in love with, but then again it was safe because he was my cousin. I was never expected to have a career.

Shirley did not pursue a career in her early years though she had a natural ability in maths and sciences. She always had good grades. After their wedding, Shirley accompanied her husband to the U.S. where he was a student at American University in Washington, DC. She too continued her studies at the same school and received a BA in art.

> One advantage of being at boarding school was the network of people we developed and, as a result of my experience, I became more independent. If I had lived in Iran it would have been a completely different life for me. I would not have stayed in Iran anyway. As far as my parents were concerned, it was good that I was away and far from trouble in a restricted environment.
>
> I never had any negative feelings of separation about being at school. Of course, having my sister and her family made it a much more pleasant situation than for most. She would come to visit and bring me Iranian food, which her maid would cook for us. She would bring pots of rice or whatever I missed. I would invite my friends and Flora would take us all out on a picnic. Because my siblings were so much older than me, separation from them was never an issue. My nephews were more like my siblings and I had them there.
>
> I had a temper and would have tantrums, especially when there was unfairness at play. I would get angry, throw a tantrum, cry and then get over it.

Roya recalls Shirley's tantrums as intense. She would get red and her involuntary tears of anger and frustration would stream down her face. However, shortly after, she would be over it. Shirley shared that as she became older she was able to manage her anger.

> My boarding school experience allowed me to feel less estranged living in England after the revolution. I felt it to be my home away from home. There was no adjustment or culture shock for me to go through. Iran will always be

my home. Yet I don't feel like a stranger in England. I would like to return to Iran one day. Even if there had not been a revolution, I would probably be living here. There were a lot of things I didn't agree with in Iran, but I would love to go back for a visit because I love the culture, the music and the country. I have hardly lived in Iran but I still feel that I'm first and foremost an Iranian.

Because Shirley is from an elite Jewish family, under the current regime she runs a risk if she returns to Iran. Her uncle and husband were among those imprisoned at the start of the revolution because of their successful business and their alleged affiliations with the previous Pahlavi government. The Islamic Republic government in later years executed her uncle. Although there are many people of Jewish faith currently residing in Iran, returning to the country is problematic for those who were considered as part of the pre-revolution *taghootis*.[4]

As a passionate Persian woman, Shirley has compensated somewhat for a forced life outside of Iran, creating her own 'kingdom' by establishing the Magic of Persia Foundation. In 2012, in an interview with a British magazine about the foundation, she stated that she began the charity as a way to encourage her son and daughter to remain connected with their cultural heritage.

> For any young person to truly discover him or herself and be able to communicate effectively with others, it is vital that they know where they come from. For example, the hospitality and generosity that is embedded in Iranian culture cannot be learned or acquired – it is inherited. I want my children to continue down the same path.

Today, through the foundation, she promotes Iranian art and culture outside of Iran and aims to make a notable contribution to its long-term advancement worldwide. Shirley continues to live in London surrounded by family and friends.

Notes

1. First in Newbury, then relocating to Oxfordshire, England, Carmel College was an elite predominantly Jewish co-educational boarding school.
2. Etefagh School Complex was a primarily co-educational Jewish day school in Tehran, which also accepted Muslim students. After the 1979 revolution, under the new Iranian constitution, Jewish schools were allowed to operate under the jurisdiction of Ministry of Education, admitting minorities only.
3. *Zan-e-Rooz* was a progressive popular women's magazine that was prohibited from publication immediately after the revolution, but was later replaced by other women's magazines.
4. *Taghooti* was a term with a negative connotation, made popular by the 1979 Iranian revolutionaries. The revolutionaries accused the wealthy members of the upper class, those associated with the royal family or the upper echelons of the government as being *taghooti*. Many *taghootis* were executed and others fled for fear of reprisal.

7
MOZART, MY FRIEND

Sheila's story
Micklefield School, Seaford, Sussex (1967–1970)

Sheila and several other friends of Soosan were daughters of National Iranian Oil Company (NIOC) executives, who arrived on the boarding school scene in the late 1960s, partly due to the increase in the price of oil and the economic boom in Iran. Micklefield seemed to have become a popular choice for the daughters of NIOC executives through word of mouth. After their separate departures from boarding school, Soosan and Sheila reconnected twenty years ago in Los Angeles. When Soosan invited her to participate in this project, Sheila agreed with the same jovial spirit and positive attitude of her youth. Her life story is, in one word, about her music. She may have blossomed as a pianist at Micklefield, but her life since then has revolved around her creative talent and her passionate commitment to playing and teaching piano. It is no surprise that the focus of her story is her music, even as she attempts to remember glimpses of her boarding school experience.

> It was about twenty years ago when I wrote a set of solo piano pieces. I then began looking for a Russian pianist to play them. At the time, I suffered from back problems and was unable to perform them myself. One reason I insisted on a Russian pianist was because Russian culture is a mixture of both East and West, and my pieces use a Persian thematic flavour in the context of classical music. The second reason was that the Russian school of pianism is perhaps the most brilliant worldwide, so it would have been the icing on the cake to have my pieces performed by one! It wasn't too long after my inquiry when I received a call from a conductor friend of mine who informed me that he had found my Russian pianist! Elated, I took my pieces to Aleksey. Little did I know that he was a composer, and not just any, but a graduate of the Moscow Tchaikovsky Conservatory – which is, if not the best, one of the top three in the world! That was quite an experience.
>
> He started by singing and analysing each one of the pieces, giving me a taste of what it meant to be in the presence of a true master! After discussing the music, we became engaged in deep discussions about the current state of music and the wrong direction it had taken. It is hard to describe how it felt to hear someone whom I so admired share my views and vision about something of such immense value to me. Once we got married, our first concern was to address our lives as musicians. We came to the conclusion that we needed to explore possible solutions as to what we could do to revive the spirit of this great art back to its original purpose. So, here we are, twenty years later!

Sheila defines herself through her music, her passion. She does not think back much to her boarding school days, but once the interview begins it slowly jars her memory.

> A long time has passed since boarding school, when I was just into my music! I was fifteen when I was sent to England. Although I was getting good grades, it was apparent that formal schooling was not for me. I was heavily into music, fashion design and painting – all of which presented an ongoing

problem for me: I was just too talented in so many areas! For a short period, I was a bit thrown off as to which direction to take. My parents agreed that I was better off not following the traditional path toward formal studies leading to university. They were worried about my future and whether indeed music or other arts were the right vocation for me. They decided to send me away so that I could explore my options and see where my talents might take me.

Prior to leaving for England, I was living with my maternal aunt and her husband in Abadan.[1] That year I ran track and field for my school and won in the 100-meter dash. I was then asked to run for the town of Abadan. I did so, and won in the province of Khuzestan. The natural progression was to participate in the national championship. So, I did, and won that too – surprisingly without *any* training! I was just bloody fast. I won two gold medals and broke the Asian record at the time. When I was asked to train for the Olympics, I declined as I knew then that it was not the direction I wanted to take. Standing on the podium with two gold medals dangling from my neck, naturally I was happy, but I did not feel proud! I now know why: because my win was the result of my natural talent, not effort. I was just naturally fast and my win felt unearned, as though to be proud of being born pretty or to being born into a rich family! After that, I was sent to England.

Having been in London for two to three weeks, exploring that wonderful city, my next stop was Mrs Hopkins' farm. Now, that was an enormous contrast to the luxurious time I spent in London. Mrs Hopkins' farm seemed to be out of the movies. I was in this large farm in Kent; a three-story-high building where the floors squeaked, the rooms were cold and the bed on which I slept was small and rather uncomfortable. Mitra (a Persian girl from Abadan, who also joined Micklefield School) was there too. I was in a house in the middle of a farm. I have dim memories of the place. I knew that it was an interim stop before going to Micklefield in Seaford. As unfamiliar as that house felt, I nevertheless loved the countryside, the weather, the rain, the beautiful white and grey fluffy clouds, and of course ... the white bread loaf, many slices of which I would devour with cream and sugar! Yummy!

Then, one day, I found myself in Micklefield. In a short period of time I had moved from Abadan to Tehran to visit my parents, from there to London accompanied by my aunt and uncle, then to the farm and then to the school. It's all a fog.

I didn't mind being in Micklefield at all. Mrs Woods was our headmistress. She was a small little lady who always had her little dogs with her. I'll never forget when I first arrived at school, I saw her in the corridor and said 'Hello, Mrs Woods'. She froze on the spot and then gave me a stern look, responding, 'Good afternoon, Mrs Woods!' And right there and then I learned my lesson!

I didn't miss my home. Well, I did a little, but then I became comfortable at school. Initially, I found it physically uncomfortable. It was too cold, my room was a little cubicle, but I knew that at school I had the opportunity to practice my piano. I found myself in the piano practice rooms all the time. Then I met Delbar (also at Micklefield) who sang and played the piano. We spent a lot of time together and bonded.

In an attempt to prompt Sheila to remember more of her experience, Soosan recalled her own experience of listening to Sheila play the piano. She described a narrow staircase from the main auditorium that would lead to a cluster of small, dark, soundproof rooms with very small windows. There was nothing but a piano and a stool on squeaky wooden floors. The rooms were hidden from the eye of the grownups; an ideal place for girls to fool around and perhaps to invoke spirits, as they often tried to do with a Ouija board!

I didn't feel much separation anxiety. I was born in Abadan and grew up there until the age of ten. My parents then moved us to Shiraz. That was a huge culture shock for me. All I remember of the four years in Shiraz was that I was constantly sick. Prior to Shiraz, I was a perfectly healthy girl. But after moving there, I caught every illness under the sun, ranging from meningitis, measles, chickenpox and mumps to a typhoid-like fever, you name it! I was as thin as a skeleton! Then at fourteen, I went back to live with my aunt and uncle in Abadan. There I regained my health.

Abadan had one of the five largest oil refineries in the world. It was an Anglo-American town with a very different atmosphere from the rest of Iran. It was something like an American suburb. I grew up with Superman comic strips, Bugs Bunny cartoons, Annie Oakley and the Flash Gordon TV series. I ate pancakes, rode my bicycle around in shorts and was in the swimming pool all day long during the summer! I loved Abadan and have the best memories of my life there. That's why the British culture was not a cultural shock to me. I was already familiar with the Western culture. My father played the guitar. After work, he would come home and teach me to play the guitar too. He had his own band. I grew up listening to Western music. My father was all about jazz, and my mother listened to Western pop music.

When I think back, I remember the cold and the physical discomfort of boarding school. I was surprised because I thought, well, this is Europe and compared to Abadan they had to be better equipped! I wanted to improve my English. I was frustrated in my language skills. To improve, I read a lot of science fiction books – which were my favourite! That is how I also entertained myself. Of course, I was also trying to adjust to my new world.

The environment was restrictive, but I went along with it. The fact that I couldn't shower every day bothered me, but as long as I was improving my piano skills, that's what counted. My piano teachers were not that good. One of them was a drunkard. He was a red-haired Irish man who stunk of alcohol and would almost fall asleep in the middle of my lessons, but I did my work. I didn't care because I just loved the fact that my music was improving. Micklefield was big on music and that was what was important to me.

As I developed my piano skills, I started to take a leadership position at school. I took charge of my own life, finishing school and then moving to London. My father asked me what I wanted to do. Since I had not given fashion design a chance, I wanted to see what that was all about. So, I applied to Lucy Clayton. They looked at my designs and immediately accepted me – I was really good! My teachers used to tell me not to leave my design drawings exposed and scattered around as my ideas could be stolen! I was only there for about a year. What bothered me the most was that I hated sewing! I couldn't tolerate it!

However, that was not why I left the world of fashion design. It was more because I missed my music so terribly. I didn't have access to a piano while in London. During that time, I let my nails grow for the first time and wore nail polish. My fingers looked pretty but strange – as though my hands were not my own!

That summer, I returned to Iran to my aunt and uncle's home in Abadan. They had a grand piano. I remember sitting at the piano, looking at my nails and thinking I can't wait to cut them so that I could play! I dashed to the drawer where they kept the scissors for Charlie and Chin Chin – their two poodles – and I used them to cut my fingernails. That felt *so* good! I sat at the piano and, oh my God, how I played and played! That experience was something else.

There was a lot of going back and forth between London and Tehran during and after my boarding school experience. At that time, I stayed at my aunt and uncle's flat in London, as I studied piano at the Royal Academy of Music with Martino Tirimo.[2] I remember when I was in Iran, Novin Afrooz,[3] a pianist friend of mine who lived both in Milan and Tehran, invited me to dinner, where I met Thomas Baldner, the German conductor who was at the time the principal conductor of the Tehran Radio and Television Orchestra. After dinner Novin asked me to play. I had just started to compose a four-hand piece, which was still unfinished. But Delbar, also a guest that evening, sat at the piano and started playing her part. So, I had no choice but to join her and play my part. When we finished, Baldner came straight to me, took both my hands, and with his dark blue piercing eyes stared straight into mine and asked me, or rather, *made* me promise to finish the piece. In return he promised to throw a party for me and invite anyone who was someone in the music world in Tehran for the occasion. We both kept our promises. Shortly after, when Joe van Didren, the newly appointed Dutch conductor of the Tehran symphony orchestra's choir, told me 'Sheila, you have five minutes to twelve! You better leave and pursue your music,' I decided it was time to seriously pursue studies in composition.

When I came to the U.S., my mother and sister were already there. Shirin, my sister, was studying at Loyola Marymount University. My mother went to the U.S. because my brother, Amir, was being treated at the Children's Hospital after contracting encephalitis at the age of eight. He was in a coma for a month with severe seizures before he finally opened his eyes. As a result of encephalitis, he was partially brain damaged. My parents had taken him all over the world to help him, and finally ended up in Los Angeles. When still in Iran, I had heard that the University of Southern California (USC) had a good school of music, so I decided to join them there. I was twenty-four when I was accepted at USC as a piano major. I began studying composition but found the experience beyond disappointing. It was horrible. While there, I won the best original film music award at Los Angeles School of Film and Music Film Festival. Yes, that was good, but I wasn't getting what I needed. I almost had a nervous breakdown.

I remember sitting in a counterpoint class when the teacher came in and asked me if I was okay. I broke into tears, very frustrated. So, I dropped out of the program after four years, I just didn't see any point in staying. I didn't want to teach at a college or university, so there was nothing for me to stay for. Immediately after, I began teaching piano privately. While doing so, I found myself writing music during the classes, to address the concepts and techniques that my students needed, and to fill in the gap of the music methods that I was using. There was so much missing, not covered in the music methodology books. So, I gradually started writing my own method. Then I met Aleksey and the rest is history!

The discipline that I was put through at boarding school has helped me a great deal. Discovering that I could stand on my own feet in a foreign country and tolerate the discomforts was a good experience for me. I became independent and I loved that. Obviously, there are a number of issues involved in terms of how the boarding school culture is experienced. One's personality is a factor – some children are more attached and some are more independent by nature. Another factor is the dynamics of the family, the relationship between the child and members of the family, the extent of their attachment, and their individual needs.

In the ancient times, the Spartans would send their children away to make warriors of them! But most children fall into the category of those who need their family, and that can create problems growing up alone and away from their loved ones. The environment and culture of the school also makes a difference. Ours was easier and less strict than some of the other schools. It's a complex issue. For me, had they sent me any earlier, say, at the age of twelve, for example, I think it would still have been the same.

I had family in London. Aunts and uncles who I visited often or their friends in Essex, Kent and London with whom I stayed during the mid-term breaks and holidays. Their friends were new to me but they were really lovely people and were always there for me. My personality is such that I don't necessarily find comfort with only people I know, but rather with those who are likeminded, and who happen to share the same values and interests as I do. That is what has always been important to me and what has made a difference in my life.

Sheila's description of the nature of her relationships with people, as well as her marriage at a later age than was considered normal at the time, raised the question of her relationship with the opposite sex.

> That didn't seem to matter so much. When in Micklefield, I would look at magazines and fantasize about life after Micklefield, of course. Perhaps it would have been nice to have boys at the school, but they would have interfered with my music. I understood that I was there to study and I accepted it. It didn't bother me. I married after forty. I had many relationships throughout my adulthood, but I couldn't really and deeply connect with any of them. I was very attractive and boys swarmed around me wherever I went, yet I never felt a deep understanding or connection with them. The only connection I found was when I was at the piano playing, communicating with Brahms, Bach and Rachmaninoff, or when driving in the car and listening to classical music. That is when I felt most at home and understood! Every piece of classical music was like a dear friend. I almost got married once, but it wasn't until I met Aleksey that I found someone who truly understood what I was all about. We talked, shared ideas and values. That is what mattered most to me. That is when I found things that I wanted to do, with someone whom I respected and admired.
>
> I don't think I have maximized or really capitalized on my potential. I could have been better – *much* better. I could have been a great painter. Painting came to me so easily. But then again, I was really good by sheer talent. Had I developed my painting talent, I would have been truly great! Just before coming to Los Angeles, I gave a concert at the Canadian Embassy – that's, of course, years ago. Listening to the recording of it today, I am amazed at how absolutely magnificent I was. So, yes, I could have done more, but my backache was the culprit. It didn't allow me to pursue my career as a concert pianist.
>
> At the boarding school, they would put me on a stretcher and take me to the Harley Street specialists for treatment. My backaches started before I went to boarding school, and my back would give out on me now and again while playing the piano. It wasn't until I met Aleksey, who treated me homoeopathically, that the pain disappeared – like magic! I remember I would be playing the piano, and suddenly one day I noticed that I've been at the piano for half an hour without any pain. I used to have to lie on the bed every ten to fifteen minutes before his treatment, but now it is gone – just like that, after all these years!
>
> I was brought up with occidental Western music. Persian music was foreign to me. The only time I heard Persian music was when I was in Shiraz during the summer holidays at my grandmother's. I became fond of folkloric Persian music. I was charmed by its simple but sincere spirit. So, I incorporated it into some of my compositions. It was when I met Aleksey that I decided to write music for voice and piano. I did so, choosing poems

from classical Persian poetry – such as Hafez[4] and Molana.[5] This was quite an undertaking and a big challenge. These pieces were much more serious and complex. I was using Persian thematic material in composing them. The treatment of harmony and formal development in them was the challenge. I gave a concert of these pieces in Beverly Hills. They were later performed at various concert halls. One day I would love to get a good recording of both the songs and my solo piano pieces.

I do miss England, though! I haven't been back. It's definitely on my 'to do' list! Aleksey and I have been so involved in our projects that we sort of entered another dimension in our lives. Now we are starting to step out. We've spent so many years on creating various programs, but we never got into the business aspect of it. To develop this methodology, Aleksey has done so much research on the scientific side of it all – in psychology, cognitive sciences, linguistics and semiotics. Now it is time to set our goals for going forward.

We are involved in two projects, both of which are programs that my husband and I have developed: the first is our Synergo Music Method – teaching music as a language system, which is done through piano, music theory and composition. The second is Kids Go Classical, which is an interactive program of musical and emotional development for children of preschool (three to four years of age) to elementary school (ten to eleven years old). In Kids Go Classical, through pantomime, act-outs, instrumental accompaniment, drawing and storytelling to recordings of classical music, which are specially selected and edited, children learn to express the emotional and imagery content of music according to the sound gestures and moods invoked by various idioms present in the music. As such, children learn to make sense out of the music they hear. We've developed our programs over the past fifteen years and have tested them with hundreds of children in various schools, organizations and privately. Now we are at a stage of preparing to put them out into the market. As for Kids Go Classical, I envision a concert show *by* children *for* children.

Sheila is a composer and pedagogue who began playing the piano at the age of seven. She currently lives in Los Angeles with her husband, Aleksey Nikolsky – a composer and a cognitive scientist. Together they train and educate students from a young age, individually and in groups, according to the Synergo Music Method, which they developed as a couple – a unique method of teaching music as a language system of emotional expression. Sheila has maintained her strong British accent. She is in her element when she speaks about her music. The memories of boarding school, though deeply buried, manifest themselves in her work ethic. She carries this toward children's overall development, teaching them to express their emotions through the music, something she herself has mastered.

Notes

1. Abadan is a southern city in the province of Khuzestan, Iran, where the National Iranian Oil Company (NIOC) and refineries operate. During the period before the Islamic Revolution, both NIOC and the city of Abadan were heavily influenced by British culture and language due to the presence of the British expats working at NIOC.
2. Martino Tirimo (1942) is a Cypriot–British pianist. He studied at the Royal Academy of Music and won the Liszt scholarship at the young age of sixteen.
3. Novin Afrooz is a renowned Iranian pianist, poet and painter.
4. Hafez is an internationally recognized fourteenth-century Iranian poet, known for his poems of love and ridicule of religious hypocrisy. Iranians often refer to Hafez's poems believing them to foretell their future.
5. Molana, more popularly known as Rumi (1207–1273), is a thirteenth-century Persian poet, jurist, Islamic scholar theologian and Sufi mystic. Known for his spirituality, he has been described as one of the most popular poets currently in the U.S.

8
WHAT IS THE USE OF CRYING?

Roxane's story
Charters Towers School, Bexhill-on-Sea, Sussex (1965–1971)

I was two years old when my father was sent on assignment from the Iranian Ministry of Economy to the U.K. My parents were married when my mother was seventeen. Soon after arriving in London, he decided that my mother should learn English. She was twenty years old at the time but claimed to be younger so that she would be accepted at a boarding school. So, I was placed into a residential nursery, Norland in Sussex. My parents would visit me on weekends and take me on an *exeat*. Increasingly, I felt uneasy leaving the nursery with my parents and wanted to go back, believing that the nursery was home and that Miss Manfred, the headmistress, was my mother.

Soon after, I don't know how soon, my mother's school became aware of her story. The regular appearance of my father for visits made it apparent that she was married. Since the school couldn't keep a married woman as a boarder, she was forced to leave. She continued her English language studies in a day school while I remained at the nursery.

We returned to Tehran after a few years. By then I had completely forgotten the little Farsi I knew as a two-year-old and had difficulty communicating with my close-knit family. It was hard for me to be accepted by my cousins, since we no longer had a common language. I had to go through a re-adaptation process, far from the nursery I knew and with an extended family who was not yet accepting of me. I was placed in the Community School in Tehran to continue my education in English.

While I was in seventh grade, my parents heard that my friend and former classmate, Roya, had gone to a boarding school in England. My father paid a visit to the school and decided that if the school was good enough for Roya's father, it was good enough for him. In those days, there was no thorough examination by the parents about whether the school suited the child's temperament, or any other deeply thought-out evaluation. Many decisions were made through fashionable trends. The trend during those years was to send your daughter for a better education to England. If the school had so-and-so rich family's daughter, then it was deemed to be a good school!

That summer, before the beginning of the academic year, my mother took me to England. We bought the uniform in preparation for my new life. She then returned to Iran and left me at a holiday home in Bournemouth until the start of the school in September. Although I already spoke English, she wanted me to get used to being in England again. Before my departure, I had already had lessons with a Miss Palmer Smith from the British Embassy, to do sums in English money (pounds, shilling, pence, guineas) and to learn British etiquette and culture. In any event, the holiday home was disappointing and I didn't particularly like being there. I was lonely and there weren't many other kids, so it was a relief when school opened and I could join my friend, Roya.

My official guardian was based in Reading, Braknell, but I don't have many memories of her. Instead, I remember my parents' friend, Mrs Eaton, who owned a bed and breakfast on Holland Road in London. If I had a problem, I would take it to her rather than my nominal guardian. The role of the Reading guardian was only a formality since the school required that the overseas girls have a guardian. I am not sure why Mrs Eaton was not my guardian other than perhaps she didn't want to take on this official role. The role of the guardian was to be the 'go to' person for the school should, for example, a student get into trouble and to pay the school tuition. At the time, sending money for tuition from Iran and contacting parents was quite difficult, so schools required a person in England to take on this responsibility. The guardian was also responsible for arranging and organizing holidays for their wards.

I liked going to Mrs Eaton. She owned a hotel in London, which was more convenient and pleasant for me. For the first couple of years, Mrs Eaton picked me up and dropped me off herself at Victoria Station, the station for the Bexhill-on-Sea train. Her bed and breakfast was where I spent half term breaks. It was also where I spent transition time between school and getting to my holiday destination, whether it was in Iran or Switzerland, where I spent many of my holidays. As I became older, I made my own way to her bed and breakfast and later to the station or the airport. It was a fairly controlled situation so there was never much time spent at Mrs Eaton's.

Crime and kidnapping was not as feared or perhaps as prevalent in those years as it is today. There was no fear of danger for young girls of twelve to sixteen taking public transport to the train station or to the airport by themselves.

In hindsight, the decisions our parents made around our lives would be inconceivable today. It wasn't only the foreign children who had these lifestyles. There were many British families who did the same for their children. I had a friend, Louise, who was the daughter of a British family based in Portugal. Other families, based in Africa, also sent their children to boarding school. This was the tail end of colonialism.

The need for boarding schools started in the 1950s. The British families based in colonies such as India, Portugal or Africa didn't have the opportunity of good educational facilities in the host countries, so they had to have a facility to send their children to avoid the disruption of their education. Also, businessmen who were based abroad, corporate employees of big companies such as Shell, BP and other oil companies, whose employees had to go to various countries and couldn't take their children, or foreign officers and military personnel who were based in odd countries; they all needed the establishment of boarding schools. Today, expatriates can place their children at schools in the host country and find excellent education systems, English or American. Forty years ago, these did not exist. There was an institutional validity for boarding schools to house children of the expatriates who couldn't, for whatever reason, have their children with them. These schools were second homes for the children. The Iranian wealthy simply followed that model. They had already begun sending their children to boarding school in the 1930s when education for women in Iran was not common, never mind sending them abroad to school. One of the first generation of boarding school girls was Dr Imran Alam. She was one of the first female obstetrics/gynaecology physicians in Iran. My own grandmother also went to a finishing school in Belgium and later to study Cordon Bleu cooking in France. We weren't the first generation.

Boarding schools in England have survived colonialism. They have metamorphosed and have had to redefine their function. Modern day boarding schools such as Seven Oaks or Cheltenham Ladies College were originally established to serve the children of the colonies, but then they had to find ways of becoming financially viable. Now they cater to the wealthy families who, for whatever reason, believe that they will receive a finer education at these establishments.

Today's schools don't have the same rules that we had in the 1960s. For example, three *exeats* per term, which was the rule at Charters Towers, don't exist anymore. Now parents can see their children as frequently as they want. Even the very traditional schools such as Eton and Harrow, which have kept their quirky traditions, allow for more access to their boarders. These changes were made ten or fifteen years ago since boarding schools were suffering as the need for them as in the times of colonialism did not exist anymore. Rich Middle Eastern families continued to send their children to the famous schools, but there was not enough demand for the schools to survive. So, they had to redefine themselves by providing more focused schools for special needs and with better sporting facilities. For example, Millfield School is thriving with their high level of sports. As a British family, if you have a child who is talented in sports, you would send your child to Millfield rather than a school in London, if you can afford it. Each of these surviving schools have found their niche. Another reason why children are sent to boarding school is because of the high percentage of broken homes. The children are arguably better off at a boarding school than at a home where they go through an emotional and tumultuous family life.

My parents genuinely thought that this was the right choice for my education. Also, in my case, during the Christmas and Easter holidays, I was sent to Switzerland to learn French and skiing. Switzerland was quite an established venue for my family since my mother's family traditionally spent time there. Many of my mother's cousins had gone to Switzerland for their schooling. During the long summer holidays from June to September, I always went back home to Iran. My parents tried to provide the best possible education and all around advancement for me.

Roxane became an excellent skier and fluent in French as a result of her holidays in Switzerland. She stayed with the same family every year and grew close to them, becoming part of that family as well.

I didn't see my parents during the year or have that many *exeats* with them. I was in contact with them through letters. Sometimes I would have *exeats* with other girls, but not that often. Occasionally, during the school year, my father would come to the U.K. on business and once, I remember he took me along with Shirley, Azy and Roya on an *exeat*. But that was rare, perhaps once or twice a year.

The question of the impact of boarding school on my life puzzles me. Given the fact that my parents sent me to the Norland nursery school at such an early age, I should, by definition, feel some separation anxiety or some other form of anxiety. I think our generation unlike our children's generation, are not accustomed to blaming our parents for things that happened to us in the past; at least I don't. I never think about judging my mother's actions towards me or blaming her for anything in the past. It's not because I understand what happened or that I do not know about Freudian therapy, which I studied at university, or appreciate psychotherapy, which I went through just to have had the experience. It's just not what our generation does. I think my mother made her best effort with our education. She thought she did her best. And my father, who was a great disciplinarian and by today's standards would be considered a horror, also did the best he could.

My father's strict upbringing of me was exceptional. Once, when I was sixteen or seventeen, I had a party during the summer holidays and had invited all my friends. At 10 p.m. he decided the party had gone on long enough and turned on all the lights, sending everyone away. No one thought this to be unusual behaviour.

I would not say today that my father's strict upbringing marked me, or that it undermined my social behaviour. But if you talk to children these days, they will bring attention to 'that day fifty-five years ago when you said those two words to me accounts for everything I do wrong in my life today'. There has been a real shift in how we look at our lives. I really believe this to be a generational phenomenon. I find that young people today are constantly griping. They feel entitled. There is this blame culture. Perhaps they see it through the media or on television; I don't know why, but for us there was no blame game. You took the hand that was given to you and you dealt with it.

Roxane's two sons are graduates of Harvard and successful in their work. They too live in London.

I don't actually remember any separation anxiety, but in my late teens I did suffer from panic attacks. I don't think it was related to my time as a boarder, because I don't see a cause and effect. In fact, both my sons occasionally suffer from panic attacks. My mother suffers from this too. More and more studies show that extreme shyness and panic attacks have a genetic basis. My mother's side of the family seems to be prone to both anxiety and panic attacks. We are anxious by nature. If you were to ask me how boarding school affected me, I would say that, contrary to assumptions, I've developed a taste for institutions! My taste for institutions such as mad houses or hospitals! I'm very happy living in hotels, dorm rooms and so on. I never have a problem with that. People complain about canteens; I wish we had a canteen here at Sotheby's.

Now that I think about it, one of the reasons my parents sent me away was that I was an only child for nine years before my brother was born. My parents thought that the chance of developing an only child syndrome wasn't a good idea – that it was important for me to socialize with other children. I was a bookworm and my father encouraged me to socialize. So, I think the social component of boarding school had a positive influence on me.

On the whole, I would say my experience at boarding school was positive. I think, however, that I missed out on generational interactions, so I'm not very good with very young or very old people because I don't have the skills. The first baby I ever held in my arms was my own son, whereas if you are living in a normal Iranian family with extended families around, you have more exposure and experience with the two ends of generations. I was missing social skills like diplomatic behaviour, being socially oriented, socially savvy, or street smart behaviours, which, had I lived at home, I would have picked up. What I did pick up at school were cultural things. For example, I discovered musical instruments at school, namely the guitar and the banjo. I learned to play them. I already knew how to play the piano.

Roxane can pick up any instrument and make music. Much like Sheila (Chapter 7), Roxane would escape to the piano room for hours, enticing her friends to join her as her small hands made magical sounds.

We had a variety of sports at school, which I would have never been exposed to had I not been in boarding school: tennis, hockey, netball and track. I enjoyed running the 800 meters. We had to participate in sports, whether we wanted to or not. The more talented girls were chosen for the teams and had to practice outside the allotted school sports period. We had house competitions, each house having their own practice time. The house sports involved the best of the house and if you weren't good enough you wouldn't be chosen to participate in them.

I developed certain habits as a result of school, which I have to this day. For example, we had to sleep with the window open, winter and summer, which I still do. This probably accounted for the breakup of my marriage, since my husband was always complaining about the cold air!

Living with all these different people and having to bathe and shower with no privacy, you lose physical inhibitions. There was a public bathroom in each house with several baths and showers. We alternated between taking a bath or shower based on assignments. The Persian girls, more accustomed to showers, often traded their bath time for a shower. Some of the Western girls shared a bath together! They filled the tub up with the allotted five inches of water, sat in it and washed together. The Persian girls found this to be disgusting. Some of us occasionally took a bath, but never with another person! For most of us, baths were not acceptable since we couldn't rinse off the soapy water before drying.

Hair washing was also assigned to once a week; allowed only in the sink not in the shower or bath. The rationale for this was that too much water would be wasted if done in the shower. The sinks had separate cold and hot water taps so we had to use a cup to mix cold and hot water and wash that way. Quite regressive.

One of my fondest memories is the really tasty unpasteurized milk coming straight from the local farms, delivered by the milkman daily. But my fondest memory was our clique of four friends. I was the only one who stayed for A-Levels. I was devastated when my other three friends left after the first year of sixth form. I lost my clique. We were one small family against the rest of the school and we got into mischief together and had fun doing so. At school my support system was my friends. Without them, it would likely have been a completely different experience for me.

Another vivid memory is when Miss McGarry did something terrible to Roya. In the later years of school, we were having individual meetings with her to discuss our future plans. Roya always wanted to be a doctor. She came out sobbing after her meeting. I later found out that Miss McGarry had told Roya that she didn't have it in her, that she would never be a doctor. I felt terrible for her then and thought it to be so unjust, the way she shattered her dream. Heather (Roya's first roommate) the smartest girl at school, later became a nurse, so there was no telling what anyone could or could not be at that time.

Roya had not recalled this experience until Roxane's interview. When she did, she realized how traumatic that experience had been for her. The memory of a young girl walking out of that office and the feeling of devastation and smallness became vivid as she listened to Roxane. She remembered the hatred she had felt for Miss McGarry at that moment, how she had crushed Roya's childhood dream. From that day on she had stopped thinking about medicine. She thought about how that conversation with Miss McGarry might have unknowingly changed the trajectory of her life. Roya also realized that in telling her story, she had let go of the bad memories of those years and remembered only the good.

After my group of Persian friends left, I shared a room with Julie in the Upper Sixth; we were the seniors. We had more authority and advantages, our rooms were nicer and we could wake up and go to bed later. We did not have to wear uniforms anymore but wore our own skirts and sweaters or twin sets and dresses for tea. The rules were much more lenient for us, yet we were in charge of enforcing them on the younger girls.

In that last year of school, the Upper Sixth, the headmistress chose two girls as Head Girls for the school. Their role was very important. The criteria with which they were chosen were based on academic accomplishment and demonstration of responsibility. It was a great honour to be chosen as a Head Girl. Miss McGarry had once scolded Roxane that had she not gotten herself into so much trouble during her earlier years, she would have been chosen as Head Girl based on her academic excellence.

> I think of myself as a fairly independent and self-sufficient person. It may be as a result of my boarding school experience or the fact that I was an only child for nine years. At the same time, I am a very selfish person, especially at this stage of my life and like to have my space and do things my way. On the other hand, the experience made me a socially competent person. Perhaps because I was taken away from my family at such an early age, it taught me to make do with what I have.
>
> My experience at school motivated me to become career minded whereas if I stayed in Iran, I probably would not have taken that route. When my friends were leaving school at first I wanted to leave the sixth form and go to the college in Switzerland with them. But my father was keen for me to finish my A-Levels. He convinced me to stay by bribing me that if I finished school, we would go on holiday together. So, I stayed and then got it into my head that I wanted to go to either Harvard, Oxford or Cambridge. I was accepted to both Oxford and Harvard and decided to go to Harvard. My father wasn't at all happy about my application to Harvard because he thought it was too far away. He thought it would be better for me to go to a university close by, maybe to Switzerland, where he himself had gone to university.
>
> The decision to go to Harvard profoundly affected my life. Many of my decisions in life have been as a result of that experience. Harvard – or Radcliffe – in the early 1970s was a very feminist environment. There was a great focus on fulfilling personal ambitions, which was in contrast to Eastern cultures, which put far greater emphasis on collective interests and family. I became quite driven and felt that it was expected of me to be self-centred. I kept studying and pushing myself, even after my children were born, when I didn't really have the bandwidth to do both. I would probably have been more relaxed about a career had I not had the Harvard legacy driving me!
>
> The Harvard experience also had an effect on both my sons, who also graduated from the school, particularly my older son. He felt he would have thrived in a more creative environment such as New York University, where he very much enjoyed his film summer school. Today he is a filmmaker. Schools like Harvard are not for everyone.

Roxane's last comment that a certain school is not for everyone brings to mind Malcolm Gladwell's book, *David and Goliath*. Gladwell argued that Ivy League schools may be detrimental to the growth of some children and their aspiration to follow their dreams and passions. He defined it as 'The Little Fish in Big Sea vs. Big Fish in Little Pond' syndrome.

> I had low self-esteem as a child since I was a very puny, sickly child, not very strong and not very attractive. Perhaps that is one of the reasons I was sent to England; my parents thought I would be better nourished and nurtured in the British countryside, doing sports daily, rather than life in a city like Tehran with its polluted air. I had seven older boy cousins, who made me feel even weaker! So, it seems natural to have had some self-esteem issues. I don't believe any of my behavioural issues are as a result of boarding school. I know that I am always trying to please and I don't know where that comes from. Could it be from trying to fit in at a young age and be accepted by the boy cousins as well as the other girls at school?
>
> My relationship with my brother is a little distant partly because of the nine-year gap. He also went to boarding school after me so we didn't grow up together. We are cordial and get along quite well. We both take care of our mother equally, but he and I are not close.
>
> I think it was a sacrifice for my parents to send me away, not so much financially but because we were such a close-knit family. I was very pampered, especially by my father, who often reminded me 'I'm not spending time with you for your benefit, so that you can have a better life'. I felt responsible; that I owed something to them because of the big sacrifice they made not to be with me. It was like he was saying to me 'Look at your mother, she's not educated. I want you to be educated and have something she never had'. So I tried to do the best with my studies, although I was a bit mischievous at school.
>
> I did feel distant from my parents and it did put me out of touch with them. I was very close to my father, but he died in my first term at university, at the age of forty-nine. So, I felt that all those years at boarding school I had been away from him and then he died. I had lost that time with him. With my mother, there has always been a certain distance, if truth be told. My brother is much closer to her in a funny sort of way. He was sent to boarding school after my father had died when she was a single mother.
>
> My closeness with my father started even before boarding school. Fathers and daughters have a different relationship. My father showed his emotions towards me more than my mother. Perhaps that's why we were close. My mother was not warm; perhaps because when she was born her father wanted a son and didn't even name her for a while. Maybe she hadn't experienced a loving relationship from her parents and didn't know how to show hers as a mother. I too don't show my emotions. I am a bit more reserved. Not that I don't feel them, but I tend to bottle them up. I think it is a learned behaviour, to protect myself.
>
> When I think of the impact of boarding school, I find that as an expat it has been extremely helpful. I have never felt pigeonholed as a Persian woman;

have never felt any prejudice as a result of being female or an Iranian. I have always felt that whatever I have wanted to do I could do. What I feel restricts me currently is my age, which is a factor for me, especially with my work at Sotheby's. Many of my colleagues are in a much younger age group. There is a lot of talk about how the workforce should be concentrated on the thirty-year-old group. That is where I feel prejudiced against now at this stage of my life.

Roxane and her husband divorced after sixteen years of marriage. She has not remarried. She sees herself as too independent and, though she may be interested in perhaps one day sharing her life with someone else, she believes that she is too set in her ways to give in to someone else's idiosyncrasies.

Roxane later continued her studies at Cambridge University, where she received her PhD in Middle Eastern History and Art. She now lives with her family in London and is currently Director of Middle Eastern Art at London's Sotheby's office. Roxane was diagnosed with cancer in 2001. She remembers how anxious she was since it was an aggressive form of cancer. She describes hyperventilating and being panicky but never once crying throughout the whole ordeal because she thought that's not useful behaviour. Although thirteen years have passed from her diagnosis, she still feels she cannot rest from the fear. She will never take her life for granted.

'What's the use in crying?' she asks.

SUMMARY

Lack of clarity and understanding of why they were shipped away to boarding school remains the dominant theme in the stories of Saghi, Dory, Shirley and Roxane and to a lessor extent Sheila. Still, growing up, they learned to resolve the culturally conflicting concepts of identity, morality and sexuality, each in her own way, driven by the implicit expectation to meet their somewhat ambiguous obligations to their parents. They cloaked their fearful self with their Persian identity as 'good girls' and 'dutiful daughters' and strived to succeed as gratitude for the sacrifices that they believed their parents had made. Childlike in the vulnerability of their dependence and fear of complete abandonment, they wished only to please and in return to be cared for. They had concluded that by being good, they would be loved, and by being emotionally strong, they would survive.

The many positive and negative effects of the experience of boarding school is evident in these stories, which reveal many levels of trauma of displacement from one's happy home to an unfamiliar and alien culture of a boarding school in England. Their reactions ranged from unquestioning acceptance of what was, to severe feelings of blame and hatred for their parents, which resulted in distance and detachment from them and those they may have once loved.

Saghi's displacement into a British family presented her with a culture shock, her initial excitement fading to frustration, settlement and ultimately acceptance towards all that she had been subjected to, including her loss of identity in becoming 'Sally'. Finally, discovering joy and freedom in France, she reconciles her cultural identity to being Saghi once again but still wondering what it would have been like to come home after school to a welcoming family, to share the day's activities, anxieties or laughter with her parents and siblings or to spend the weekends, going on road trips to the fun places that had left happy memories?

Dory's need for belonging and affection is demonstrated in her longing for communication and connection to the outside world. Receiving letters was not only a way to feel connected with her family, but proof that she was not alone or forgotten, that she was indeed loved. Her feelings of loneliness and abandonment were occasionally and temporarily relieved by the ritual of receiving mail from home and the jolly sense of involvement, but the letters simultaneously alerted her to a deep feeling of emptiness in her heart. The geographical distance from her family caused an irretrievable detachment from her parents, leaving her with the belief that her parents truly did not care for her or her siblings.

For Shirley, the urgency to learn a foreign language in an attempt to effectively communicate only facilitated a rebellious performance that exuded confidence and vitality. Once in a foreign distant land, she quickly developed different ways of recreating her own world. She resisted 'pulling up her socks' to maintain the independent, resourceful and resilient personality she once had at home, and she continued to defy authority. She developed a long-standing entourage of friends and associates and stayed true to a self with strong values for equality and tolerance, reinforced by the lack of racism and bigotry as her natural interactions with others.

Whether Sheila took refuge at the piano or whether she took advantage of her creative gift and abundance of natural talents with which she was endowed, she has given meaning to her life in ways that have minimized the impact of her years at boarding school. Growing up with all the trials and tribulations of adolescent exploration, Sheila's passion for music and her choice for integration of Eastern and Western sounds are an expression of an emotional voice of a cultural foundation that is deeply embedded in her identity as a Persian musician.

Roxane, a Harvard and Oxford graduate and talented Middle Eastern scholar, laments not being with and connecting with her extended intergenerational family members. She wonders about how things would have been different had she had a normal life growing up with her parents' love at home? Her story portrays how she developed a resilience to withstand negative life events, how she coped and endured in the face of major obstacles and feelings of vulnerability, and how she learned to keep her emotions at bay and project a strong sense of assurance. Working at Sotheby's, she wishes for a canteen rather than a restaurant as she claims a love for institutions with their imposing and often confining structures but a place where people function effectively.

PART III
Lives unknown

INTRODUCTION

When one door of happiness closes, another opens; but we often look so long at the closed door that we do not see the one which has been opened for us.

Helen Keller[1]

Human beings are often burdened by the enduring fantasy of what life could or should have been. Cherishing the search, we embarked on a journey to know and to find meaning, not as much to explain the past, but rather to understand the challenges of the present as a way of orchestrating a positive future. We delved into our youthful memories and feelings in order to better understand what we have done or failed to do as women in the many roles we have played as daughters, mothers, wives and as professionals. As our lives continue to unfold, what could have been will remain a compelling mystery to us, even as our reflections shed light on our past actions and the decisions that we made. Yet, our compelling stories helped us understand and, in some ways, process our youthful separation from parents, appreciate our lifetime friendships with other girls and pave our path toward the next cycle in our lives. How each of us engaged with our stories has much to do with who we are today at the time we tell our story and what we choose to remember.

Emotions are governed by thoughts, but thoughts, beliefs and assumptions can be challenged and changed for the purpose of improving one's psychological well-being and resilience. As we give voice to our stories, we struggle with the emotional residue of our experience, perhaps denying our feelings and thoughts and unable or unwilling to talk about or share them freely. Children vary in their temperament and sensitivity towards their parents and the environment that influences them. But clearly boarding was a traumatic experience for many of us because our separation from parents coincided with key developmental stages at ages five, eight or as adolescents. We were told that we were special for being sent away to boarding school, but at the moment of loss, when our parents left us alone at a train station, on the doorsteps of a strange home or in front of a large institution, we could not have felt special. Instead, at that moment, we found ourselves alone, part of a huge strange world where we had to manage our lives as adults. We had to grow up overnight!

As is explained in the documentary film *The Making of Them*[2] there is a 'double bind':

> Mom and Dad say they love me, but they are sending me away. But if they love me why are they sending me away? If I show I don't like it, they will be disappointed and if they are disappointed maybe they won't love me; so I won't show them I don't like it. Or … if I don't like it maybe there is something wrong with me and that's why they sent me away!

We emerged from this double bind trap in different ways but for the most part accepting of our place in the real world. There are those of us with more difficult temperaments and less agreeable personalities who appear to have been more vulnerable to parental absence, believing that boarding school experience played a pivotal role in preventing us from achieving our potential and that it had a significant impact on our life satisfaction and sense of happiness. Whether we internalized the boarding school experience as traumatic or motivating, whether we complied, rebelled or identified as a casualty, we have all developed a way to cope with adversity.

Our struggle with adversity and the manner in which we chose to cope with it, helped us develop skills useful in successfully negotiating a variety of challenges faced in our adult lives. Almost collectively, we believe that our youthful British experiences prepared us to forge through a revolution that disarrayed and upturned our lives and that of our families. We had formulated the strength and perseverance to restart our lives wherever we landed. After all, we had learned to survive and, in many cases, thrive from an early age. The lives we chose to live after the revolution and the careers we later pursued were in part influenced by what we inherited from our boarding school education. While at school, every moment of our day was accounted for: sleep, meals, lessons, sports – all were scheduled with minimum flexibility or freedom. As such, many of us became high achievers with little aptitude for downtime enjoying 'doing' rather than 'being'.

Notes

1 www.goodreads.com/author/quotes/7275.Helen_Keller. Retrieved 16 February 2017.
2 *The Making of Them* (1994), a British TV documentary filmed in September 1993. It is about young boys in boarding prep school. This is the earliest example of a documentary about 'modern' boarding schools. www.youtube.com/watch?v=2uRr77vju8U, retrieved 8 April 2015.

9
PLAYING NICE

Soosan's story
Micklefield School, Seaford, Sussex (1965–1970)

I arrived in the U.K. as a twelve-year-old, following in the footsteps of my older sister. Earlier, I had said goodbye to my parents and family and, along with my sister Sudi, who was returning to the U.K. after a summer vacation in Iran, boarded the Iran Air flight for Heathrow Airport. As excited as I was about joining my sister whose presence I had missed terribly, I was more excited to discover life at school in England. To my delight, and at the insistence of my mother, the decision was made for me to accompany my sister back to the U.K. I had overheard my brother-in-law suggest that as the youngest child, I would not survive being away from my mother. There and then I had made up my mind that I would prove them wrong and never go back.

I remember standing there at the Victoria Station train platform, nervous while trying to look comfortable in my formal, recently acquired school uniform. Wearing my new straw boater hat, I would sneak stolen looks to absorb all that was going on around me. The platform was slowly becoming crowded with girls arriving, boarding the train and screaming with laughter and joy at the sight of familiar faces of old friends. It had been an exciting and unimaginable three days since my arrival in London. Now, thousands of miles away from home, I was standing obediently next to the woman I had come to know in the last three days as my guardian – Mrs Peck, waiting for her instructions. There was no other familiar or welcoming face, so all I could do was simply look and absorb. Who were these girls? How were they dressed? What were they saying to each other? I could not speak English and only imagined, in my youthful, spirited head, how much fun they were having. I was not worried about being away from home as much as the thought of how quickly I could fit in, learn to become like them, one of them. I imagined it was going to be fun, exciting, perhaps even liberating. I was going to enjoy all of this without trepidation about what lay ahead.

Years later, when I asked my mother why I was sent to boarding school, she professed that she wanted to be fair; she believed that whatever was done for my sister had to be done for me. I suspect that the decision to send my sister to boarding school was considered to be a privilege bestowed on her; a privilege that I too was granted two years later. I cannot help but wonder about the emotional and financial cost of this privilege. What had we, our parents and us, given up in return for receiving a Western education? Did other girls see their departure as a privilege – a sacrifice made by their parents? Did our parents, in their attempt to be fair, forget to see us as individuals with our unique needs? Should we have had a voice in determining our path forward at such an early age?

The flight, my first to London, was not memorable except for the many questions that I had for my sister who herself had, perhaps, experienced the same excitement two years earlier. Now, she was returning to school after a much anticipated summer vacation and family visit. The thought of being with Sudi at the same school was in itself exhilarating. I believed that she had been sent to the U.K. because she was special. I would spend my time at boarding school and perhaps the rest of my life proving that I too was 'special', not knowing exactly what that meant or whether in fact this rationalization was only a figment of my imagination.

On arrival in London, our guardian, Mrs Peck, met us at the airport. She was a tall, impeccably dressed woman, whose stern but kind eyes quickly sized me up and welcomed me along with my sister. I was relieved to find her speaking in Farsi since I assumed everyone spoke English in England! I still remember the scent of Mrs Peck's perfume and her confident, authoritative presence demanding instant respect. We were taken to her home in Kew Gardens, Richmond, where we spent the next two nights. There, to my surprise and to what must have been a disappointing and somewhat fearful announcement, I learned that I was not going to the same school as my sister. Mrs Peck, in her infinite wisdom, had decided that I needed to be separated to avoid depending on my older sister. In retrospect, this was a critical decision that fundamentally impacted my experience at boarding school and who I was to become as an adult. Our schools turned out to be very different and so were our experiences of days spent away from our parents. The boarding school environment affects children differently. In the case of my sister and I, we were touched as much by the culture of our schools and the individuals who influenced us, as our own unique personality traits.

The day after our arrival, Mrs Peck and I took the train back to the big city for a shopping expedition at Barkers. There, two older Iranian girls, Simin and Shirin, joined us. They paid little attention to me, but I was intrigued by them as they spent time around the cosmetic stalls trying on different makeup items. I don't remember seeing them again in later years, but that day we spent hours together following Mrs Peck and the shop floor assistants, as they collected items from what appears to have been the most extensive shopping list, managed by Mrs Peck.

My uniform list included white and green underpants, white and green knee-length and ankle-length socks, green sport shorts and green skirts, white sport T-shirts as well as white long-sleeve dress shirts. Wasn't a tie something only men wore? And why did we all have to wear the same colour underwear? Who was going to see it? And the shoes, they were ugly and masculine, not the fancy footwear that had caught my eyes earlier in the store! While I wandered about in amazement, Mrs Peck made sure that everything was the right size and that they fit perfectly. And this was just our everyday uniform! We had a whole different wardrobe for formal events like travelling, outings or Sundays, when everyone went to church, and yet still another set for sports. All this and a beautiful blue metal trunk with golden locks to carry it all! I could not wait to get into my uniform.

I do not remember shopping for clothes with my mother before leaving Iran. She, along with my aunt, were expert seamstresses. All our clothing, for my twin cousins and me, were made at home, except for the occasional items that my father would bring back from his trips to Europe. The other exception was when we were taken shopping for the traditional annual family shopping for *Nowruz*[1] to buy brand new dresses, socks and shoes as was customary. But this was different. The number of items that we purchased and the bags that we carried far exceeded my imagination. How could I not feel and be special? At least until I saw hundreds of other girls with the same clothing!

> Now, fully dressed in my new uniform, identical to all the other girls, I was ready to board the train when Mrs Peck introduced me to another Iranian girl, Delbar. Finally, someone I could speak to and share stories with. Delbar was at the station with her brother, who quickly left us after handing over his sister to Mrs Peck. Delbar was a lively young girl who seemed to know her way, having joined the school a year earlier. I liked her. We sat together and shared stories for the next two hours until we arrived at Seaford. There, the buses were waiting to take us to Micklefield School. Driving along the rocky seashore, I could not imagine what the school would look like. I watched in amazement as we passed the Seven Sisters cliffs and turned in on a dirt road toward the entrance. The Seven Sisters are a series of seven chalk cliffs by the English Channel in Seaford. I later found that these cliffs were within walking distance of Micklefield, serving as our playground on weekends when we were taken for walks or a swim.
>
> My mind was cluttered with random thoughts. What will my room be like? Will I have to share it with other girls? What would be expected of me? Will my trunk be there when I arrive? I had committed to being a dutiful daughter so whatever was in store for me, I aimed to simply put my shoulder to it.

On arrival, we were greeted by teachers and guided by a senior student to our cubicles in the dorm. We were given our daily schedule and instructions on when to be ready for dinner and what to wear.

> All of this must have been a fog as I could not understand the language and hence relied on Delbar to tell me what I was supposed to do. It must have been a strange feeling not being able to follow the conversations of others, but somehow it didn't matter. The smiling faces and helping hands of the other girls were enough to make me feel welcomed. Mrs Peck's instructions were that I carry my dictionary with me everywhere and, not only that, but to make sure that whenever I spoke, I used 'thank you' and 'please'; two words that I now know I must have overused and misused on many occasions, as I grasped for ways to communicate during those early days. How would knowing the language have impacted me differently in those early days?
>
> Life at school evolved as I learned to speak English and navigate my way through the different subject matters with different teachers. I had entered the school in the fourth form and needed to quickly master both the language

and the topics to prepare for my O-Levels in the fifth form. I remember feeling traumatized after failing a maths test. I was good at maths so lack of English fluency should not have held me back! It was only after the form teacher, the lovely Mrs Peyton, showed me my work, saying she could not understand what I had written, that I realized I had inadvertently completed the work in Farsi. No wonder she couldn't make sense of it! Thankfully, she allowed me to recalculate everything in front of her, this time in English, so that I could receive the grade A that I deserved. As I became exposed to different subjects, I was able to quickly choose the ones I wanted to focus on for my O-Levels. I decided that geography and biology were not an option, not because I wasn't interested or didn't have the aptitude but because I simply did not enjoy the teacher, Ms Hutchinson! She was a single woman of strong personality, with an aggressive approach to life, who went swimming in Seaford Bay every morning even in the cold of winter! I was afraid of her.

Aside from my focus on academics, I was also quick to find friends from all over the world. I naturally mixed and mingled with others because I was curious and anxious to learn whatever it was I had to learn. I was adventurous with an openness to new experiences or, as my family had come to label me, *sheitoon* (mischievous or naughty). I was not rebellious, though I found the strict boarding school structure and listening to authority challenging. Early on, I seemed to have found a thrill in doing what was forbidden and acting against the rules, such as walking barefoot when we were required to wear slippers or leaving the lights on beyond the regular hours, only to turn them off quickly upon hearing the matron's footsteps, climbing trees to pick fruit or even climbing down the fire escape to join others at the bowling alley outside the town.

Needless to say, my readiness to make mischief often resulted in severe detention. My first punishment was learning the names of the British kings and queens and the dates of their reign! Memorizing was easy for me because that is how we were trained to learn in Iran. But for a twelve-year-old who could not speak English, pronouncing the names and the dates was a different story! I took it all in my stride. I was doing what I wanted, even if it meant missing my favourite show on television, 'Top of the Pops', by spending weekends washing dishes in a smelly kitchen! I was not a wimp. So, the other girls didn't dare pull pranks on me. Perhaps the horror stories I had heard from my sister, who had warned me about young girls' cruelty, had indirectly helped to prepare me.

Over the years, I learned to share a room with four or five other girls and understand, at a personal level, about growing up British. Privacy took on a different meaning at boarding school when you had to share a room with others. I witnessed how English girls also had parental expectations to meet; how they too missed being with their family. I learned about deviant behaviours that would get girls in trouble, such as stealing, lying, dealing with unwanted pregnancy and then the gin and hot baths that were used to cause a miscarriage. As time passed, as a sixth former, I shared a room with only one person and later had an individual room. As an introvert, I cherished having my own space where I could finally withdraw into my own world, create imaginary boyfriend stories, look at my family photos, write letters and even occasionally cry myself to sleep without the watchful eyes of roommates.

My immediate circle of friends eventually expanded to include Martha from Uganda, Claude from France, Barbara from the U.K. and Krista from Germany. The interaction of the different cultures among the girls was as natural as our being there was unnatural. Our childhood curiosity about differences found satisfaction in the common emotions and feelings that we shared as roommates, classmates and friends.

The arrival of four other Persian girls at the school was, however, significant. There were many occasions when I missed home or felt sorry for myself for being away from family and former friends. At such times, the Iranian girls in the school provided me familiarity and comfort. Our support for each other was our bulwark against homesickness, enabled by our ability to empathize with each other.

I remember during daily break the mail would be distributed among the students, I would wait eagerly to see the distinct blue airmail letter/envelope among the pile of letters, hoping that it was for me. Mail was slow, but I was desperate for the letters from my mother telling me about their life back in Iran or letters from my father with spelling and editorial corrections of my Farsi. Occasionally, after a long absence of letters from Iran, to cure homesickness, Soheila (Chapter 11) and I would spend our prep time in the library, writing letters to each other and putting it in the mailbox. That way, we were sure to receive mail the next day.

It was a special feeling receiving mail, perhaps a confirmation that we were remembered and loved. There was also the occasional care package that would arrive from Iran with pistachio nuts and other Iranian snacks. Since we were not allowed to keep food in our room, we would very quickly share the food among the girls or make a dismal attempt to hide it from the matrons' daily inspection of our rooms. Then there were the occasional phone calls from my sister Sudi who was at The Grove School in Surrey. I could not wait to hear from her and tell her all about what was going on.

After five years of what I generally recall as an *amazing* experience, I left Micklefield in 1970. Roya asked me why I describe my experience as amazing. I guess whenever I look back to those years, I am reminded of a young, spirited Persian girl who learned not to look back and brood about the past. Moving forward was my goal. Little time was spent worrying or contemplating about what I left behind. I was there to study hard and to make my parents proud. I did. I was also going to enjoy my life despite its challenges. I did. I enjoyed my father's total trust and felt empowered to make my own decisions, such as having my own bank account, managing my own expenses and making my own travel plans.

The notion of being taken for granted for doing well and being 'OK' can be a double-edged sword. I had mastered the art of taking care of myself early on in life, not because my parents didn't care for me, but because there was always something or someone else they needed to attend to and because they trusted and believed that I would be able to fend for myself. It is gratifying to know that your parents trust you and your judgments because all I ever heard was that 'we don't need to worry about Soosan'. It gave me a sense of accomplishment to prevent them from ever having to worry about me. At the same time, I learned not to give myself the permission to be vulnerable, to express emotional or financial needs for fear of disappointing those who trusted me. The resulting behaviour is that I simply keep moving on to meet the expectations in order to fare well!

> Success was defined, evident from my letters to my parents, as satisfying their expectations; expectations that were never defined explicitly in terms of an outcome. As far as my mother was concerned, boarding school was about having a good education so that I could stand on my own feet. As far as my father was concerned, it culminated in having a good education to make him and a potential husband proud. On her departure for boarding school, my sister recalls receiving a framed calligraphy in Farsi from our parents that said *On Chenan Bash Keh Pedar va Madarat Arezou Darand* (Translation: 'Be what your parents wish you to be'). The British boarding school was expected to make my parents' dream come true. I never questioned their dream. It naturally became mine.

An old friend recently reminded me that on leaving Iran, in response to her question on why I was being sent to England, I had responded '*keh adam shavam*'. The translation is 'to become civilized' but the common meaning implied by the statement is 'to conform, to become obedient'. At least, this was my youthful understanding of the purpose of boarding school. I have since discovered using the same expression repeatedly in my letters to my parents and in my journal entries. I am not able to recall how I came to adopt this particular phrase other than I must have heard some adult in the family saying so. It seems that I have used it to give myself a purpose, a goal to strive for. Whether the expression indicates conformity or whether it reflects my parents' belief in the superiority of Western values, it seems to have provided me with a rationale for being away from home. Clearly, at twelve years of age, the importance I had given to it was designed to please my parents by learning as much of the new ways as possible. With that came the acceptance of the new life and the belief that I was benevolently placed there and must therefore adapt and meet any and all challenges. And so, the occasional punishment for disobeying the rules, the humiliating experience of acknowledging bad behaviour at morning assembly in front of hundreds of other girls and teachers, the lonely long weekends when English girls returned home or the desperate need for a friendly adult of the same sex to discuss 'girl' stuff slowly became part of life's obstacles that I had to overcome to achieve a higher goal.

England became home. The friendships with girls from diverse cultures opened my eyes to what was going on in the world at the time. The 1960s were a time of tumultuous change in England and abroad. Although we were somewhat buffered against these changes, there was a curiosity about the world around me. My best friend, Martha, with whom I frequently listened to Desmond Dekker's music, inspired me to learn about the civil rights movement. As a student of history, I was fascinated with the American Civil War and in particular with the Civil Rights movement in the U.S. I read Dr King's autobiography and was in awe of his courage. My best friend in Iran was Jewish. We had grown up together, yet I knew little about the Jewish experience until I became captivated by Anne Frank's diary. Inspired by her words, like many other girls, I began to keep a journal of my own.

However, it was less the political and more the social changes in England that excited me as a teenager. Beatle mania was happening and though my favourite singer was Cliff Richard, I could not wait to go to a Beatles concert. I never did. The miniskirt rebellion of Mary Quant and the rise to stardom of Twiggy and Lulu were well underway. As the miniskirt fashions began to show up in London's Chelsea boutiques, my pleated school skirt got shorter and shorter, rolled up at the waist!

Holidays were spent with the Nicklen family in Bournemouth. They were a middle-class couple with two girls, Judy and Katherine. While Judy, as the older sibling, had the freedom to stay out late at night, Katherine, along with my sister and me, were brought up under Mrs Nicklen's strict rules. Mrs Nicklen presented the perfect picture of a housewife and a mother. She served us tea and biscuits in bed, took us bird watching on weekends, read us stories and attended to Mr Nicklen, who was retired and who spent most of his time at home reading and smoking a pipe on his reclining chair. Drinking eggnog and decorating the tree on Christmas Eve, opening the presents in our pyjamas and pulling large crackers at the dining table, serving turkey and plum pudding, are among the many Nicklen traditions that I have continued to share with my own children and grandchildren.

> I spent one of my best Christmas holidays with my English friend Barbara. She owned her own horse. That winter, we woke up at five in the morning, shovelled the barn, fed the horses, brushed them and went for rides in the woods. The following summer, Barbara visited Iran with me as a guest of my family. Iran was prospering as a result of the large inflow of oil revenue and the Shah's determination to move Iran toward Western values. Returning to Tehran for the holidays wearing our 'mini-jupe' or 'maxis' on the streets was exciting in as much as my fashion conscious girlfriends were able to follow suit. Barbara and I enjoyed the luxuries that our life in Iran had to offer with teenage pool parties and chauffeur-driven beach trips to the Caspian Sea. I believe that her experience in Iran was as novel as mine had been while living with her family in Surrey. She was treated special because she was *khareji*

(foreign) and received much attention from my family members. When the time came to go back to school, Barbara was reluctant to leave Iran. My mother, to my disappointment, suggested that she stay behind while I alone returned to England.

The rapid change of the 1970s in the Iranian social environment and the perception of freedom excited my mother enough to encourage me to return home after completing my A-Levels instead of going to Switzerland, which was the original plan. I agreed. With my trunk packed, this time with new clothes of my own choice, presents and souvenirs for my family and a new tune that signalled permanent departure from England, I returned home. Within less than a year of my return, at age seventeen, I was a second-year student at Damavand College[2] and engaged to be married. My mother was against my marriage because she thought I was too young. But there was no freedom for a young girl in Iran and in any case all I dreamed of was to get married and have many children. My marriage lasted for many years and even survived a year of residency as an MBA student while my one-year-old daughter was taken care of by my older sister. It did not survive the aftermath of the 1979 revolution.

In 1981, I found myself back in England, separated from my husband, this time with my two children, ages six and two. Prior to this, due to my father-in-law's illness, we had moved and lived in the second-floor apartment of my in-laws' house in Iran. Most of my belongings, including my cherished blue trunk filled with personal books, diaries and memorabilia, were stored in the basement of their house. My mother-in-law, fearful of revolutionary raids and unbeknownst to me, attempted to purge the house of artefacts associated with being *taghooti*, used my trunk to ship everything out of their house. For the first time, the absence of the 'trinket' trunk in my life brought up familiar emotions of separation and yet, with its absence, it seemed to herald a new tune. I had learned not to brood about the past and this was a reminder to keep moving forward.

In 1988, after an amicable divorce, my children and I became Canadian and began yet another phase of life away from my birthplace. I had studied business with the hope of working with my father in Tehran. When I graduated with an MBA, my father's response was that downtown Tehran was no place for a woman to work. Years later, extensive business experience downtown on Toronto's Bay Street and New York's Wall Street compensated for my father's rejection. Now, as a university educator with a doctoral degree, as a mother and a grandmother, there are still lingering questions about lived experiences of boarding school, the emotional cost of independence and the challenge of breaking the protective shell of vulnerability, wondering how I can thrive on change and yet be constantly in search of stability in my life?

I no longer have my trunk, which is now replaced by a steady profession and stable life, but I do wonder why so many of us formed such an attachment and held onto the fond memories of our trunk, the one object that seemed to remain constant in our lives.

Notes

1 *Nowruz* (New day) is the first day of Spring, celebrated as the Iranian New Year. There is a tradition of buying and wearing new clothes for the celebrations.
2 Damavand College, formerly known as Iran Bethal, was a private institution of higher education for girls, offering a liberal arts undergraduate degree. Many devout Iranians not wanting to send their daughters to mixed universities or those who had returned from foreign assignments, sent their daughters to Damavand. After the 1979 revolution, the college was amalgamated into what is now Allameh Tabatabai University.

10
IT COULD HAVE BEEN

Shoreh's story

Godstowe School, High Wycombe, Buckinghamshire (1957–1962)
Hargrove Abbey, High Wycombe, Buckinghamshire (1962–1968)

Shoreh and Roya met at the American College of Switzerland and became close friends. They continued their friendship while living in Iran and later in the U.S., where they get together with Azy, Shoreh's former college roommate, regularly. This interview was done in Los Angeles at one of these reunions.

> I was sent to Godstowe boarding school in High Wycombe with my sister Guilda when I was six and she was seven and a half. I don't know how my parents found this school. They just sent us off to a guardian, Mrs Fox, who lived in High Wycombe. They were the only family in town who accepted both of us. The other families wanted to separate us but my father insisted that we had to be together wherever we went. I presume having both of us would have been too much of a burden for the families. Mrs Fox was not only our guardian but her house was where we returned during the holidays when we did not go back home.

As she begins to narrate her story, Shoreh is surprised by the tears flowing down her cheeks. She acknowledges that this is the first time she has shed tears thinking about her past and attributes it to pent up sadness.

> I can't imagine why my parents would send two young children away to some unknown person's house at such a young age?

Attempting to hold back tears, she abandons the thought of her parents and continues with the story, but her sentiments again raise the question of why parents send children to some faraway school for education at such a young age.

> Mrs Fox had three children, Jane, Michael and Brian. Her husband was the headmaster of a local school. Jane was a year younger than me. The house rules were very strict – no television and only classical music allowed. Our main entertainment was reading, though sometimes we kept ourselves busy with knitting. Guilda and I became friends with Jane and introduced her to Coca-Cola and pop music, to her parents' chagrin. The additional income the Fox family earned from our boarding fee allowed them to send Jane to a public school (which in England refers to a paid private school). England was going through a period of austerity at the time and the Foxes were a middle-class family, not well off financially. Christmas celebrations, for example, were very simple with a light meal. One time Mrs Fox's wealthy sister took us out for a meal and that was a very special occasion for us!
>
> Mrs Fox was cold and unemotional. Guilda and I didn't enjoy our stay. We always felt like an outsider. There was no warmth or appearance of caring for us, these two foreign six- and seven-year-old girls. We were just a source of income for them. We passed the time during our stay, while looking forward to the end of the holidays when we would return to school. Like many other girls, once we left England we never looked back or felt the need to reconnect with this family again.

To get to High Wycombe, we would go to Marylebone train station in London and a representative from our school would pick us up. When we were older we would go to London and stay with my older cousin, Farhad – that was a treat, that was freedom! The first time I actually spent time in London was when I was eighteen. To this day, I don't travel well; train stations and airports depress me.

At school, we were the only foreigners and considered quite exotic. We didn't speak any English when we arrived, but within a few weeks we were both speaking the language. I don't have much memory of that early period, but I do remember that the headmistress's daughter befriended me and we started communicating with a language of our own. She was my advocate. I hated the food. You can imagine coming from the food in Iran to English food! My friend would tell the headmistress: 'Shoreh doesn't like the food; you have to give her fruit'. Of course the answer was: 'She has to eat whatever we put in front of her'. (Fruit was an expensive commodity in England at the time and not often provided to us at school.) The headmistress would ask her: 'How do you know? She doesn't speak English'. And her daughter would say: 'We know how to talk to each other'. She always tried to help me out. But I had to adapt.

Shoreh was a finicky eater as a child and continues to be so to this day. She eats a lot of fruit and vegetables. Even when healthy food was not as fashionable as it is today, Shoreh was health conscious. This passion for healthy eating brought about the writing of her cookbook, *Camelot's Kitchen*, inspired by her bunny rabbit Camelot and his eating habits, which Shoreh considered similar to her own! Although she appears shy and reserved, she is extremely creative with an intriguing quality and charm that is almost undetectable.

My sister was always the rebellious one. From the beginning, she managed to find the naughty girls at school. Within one week of our arrival, she decided to run away. The night before her escapade she came to me and said:

'Shoreh, I'm going to run away'.
'What about me?' I reacted, petrified.
'Don't worry; when I get to London I will send for you'.
'Do you know where London is?' I asked.
'Yes, my friends know!'

She then packed up her bundle – just like you see in the cartoons – and off she went with her friends. At 5 a.m., the headmistress came to my bed:

'Wake up, wake up. Where is your sister?'

Guilda had warned me before she left,
'Don't you dare tell them where I am going'.
The headmistress insisted: 'I know she told you where she has gone'.

> I didn't dare say anything but within half an hour they had caught her. This was an easy catch; a couple of seven-year-olds wandering around the town of High Wycombe! The town *was* the school. There was nothing else. That's about the only vivid memory I have, because of the panic Guilda had caused. When they were brought back to school, they were punished and had to stay in their beds for the rest of the day!
>
> There was one Persian girl, Maryam, who also came to our school, but she didn't follow us to Hargrove, the secondary school, as the other girls did. There were a few international girls, including those from Africa. All my friends were English.

Shoreh carries on with her story but appears preoccupied with the question of why her parents had sent her to boarding school.

> I don't remember much more about that period, until we went to the secondary school. Once I asked my father why he sent us (not my mother because she wasn't involved in the decision) and he said because he wanted to make sure we had the best education and this school was one of the best in England. But I think there was another underlying reason. My uncle, six years my father's senior, had gone to school in England. He had finished the Polytechnic University in Iran, a very prestigious engineering school, and then continued his studies at Cambridge University in the U.K. When it was time for my father who had planned to go to Manchester University, the Second World War had begun, preventing him from continuing his studies abroad. He felt deprived and short-changed that he had not had the same opportunity as his brother; he was very competitive. According to my mother, before we were sent my father had tricked her telling her we would go for a couple of years, but of course it ended up being until we were adults.
>
> Hargrove, our secondary school, had excellent academic standards. The teachers were exceptional. I focused on taking languages, French, Italian and German, for my O-Levels. However, when the time came for the exam, there was a conflict because Italian and German exams were scheduled on the same day. It was unusual for a student to take so many languages simultaneously. So, I was placed in quarantine while sitting for the second exam the next day. I had a gift for languages and the headmistress, Ms Fisher, was convinced she could get me into the best universities of England.
>
> I have fond memories of Miss Fisher. She seemed to understand us. She was an overpowering six-foot-two-inch woman; all the girls were afraid of her and would shake as she passed us in the corridors. She was the niece of the famous Archbishop Fisher and she had previously been the headmistress at a school in Kenya. Miss Fisher was forced to leave when all the whites were advised to leave because of the Mau Mau uprising in Kenya. She recalled the story to us:

One day as I was smoking a cigarette, wondering what my life would be like after Kenya, I saw in the mirror that the houseboy was coming behind me with a knife. He had been told to kill every white person he saw. Being the person that I was, I turned and said with authority, 'James, what are you doing, drop the knife immediately'. He dropped the knife and apologized saying: 'I'm sorry, I'm sorry; I was told to do this'. I didn't sleep all night and the next morning got on a plane to the U.K. and ended up at Hargrove.

Although I enjoyed returning home for the holidays, I didn't really have any emotions towards my parents or my brother. It was sad. I didn't really know them. My boarding experience has affected my ability to show my emotions towards anyone, except for my son once he was born. It is also difficult for me to accept being loved; I don't trust it and question 'Why do you love me?' It made it difficult for me to bond with my first husband or my present one. I don't think I have ever felt romantic love. I envy the people who have. I did love one man in college. It was innocent and spontaneous; pure emotion. It was what you could call unconditional love; maybe it can only happen at that age. So much wasted time and emotion. So much I could have given, offered and received.

Despite the sexual revolution of the 1970s and the relative freedom found in college, most of the Iranian girls continued to be sexually reserved. It had been ingrained in many of us to stay virgins until we were married. It took a few years to get used to the idea of this newfound freedom and to become sexually liberated once we were old enough to do so. For some, that time has never come!

Teachers were usually spinsters; their fiancés or husbands having been killed during the War. I do remember a chemistry teacher who was as such. I also remember my German teacher, Miss McNab, and Madame Ferrier, my French teacher, who was elegant and beautiful. The minute we stepped in her class, we were not allowed to speak any language other than the language of that class.

I never experienced prejudice while at school, although when the colonies split up, prejudice became a little more prevalent in England. Enoch Powell's daughter was at our school. He was the British Parliamentarian who was very outspoken and was famous for calling to close the gates against immigrants and not let them in. Most of the rest of the members of parliament were saying: 'How can you not let them in, they are a part of the Empire'. He was very unpopular because of this sentiment and we could tell that his daughter felt uncomfortable because of her father's views.

But we Persians fascinated the English. We were the girls from a faraway land and were different and exotic in their eyes. I had three best friends at different stages of my schooling, Vivien and two Janes. All of them were accustomed to being at boarding school from an early age. Jane had three other sisters, one was at the school and the two younger ones were still at home in Kenya, where the family lived and her father worked as a teacher. They were a product of the colonization, which is why boarding schools became popular in England. Jane was accustomed to being away from home. I had a lot of fun with Jane, although she was a terrible influence on me, because she was so naughty. The other Jane had a house in Montand in the south of France where she invited me for one holiday. That is when I discovered that there was another world outside of boarding school. Vivien came from a conservative family. Her father was a doctor and she later became one too.

There were ten houses at our school, each had a different name, different colour theme and located in a different area on the grounds. I was assigned to Shelbourne, which was one of the three houses on top of the hill. We stayed in the same house for the duration of our education. Each age group was in a separate dormitory. Each house was like a family with girls of different ages and cultures. We wore the tie colour of our particular house. Shelbourne's tie colour was blue. From our houses to the main school was three-fourth-of-a-mile walk. We basically had the hardest walk to the main building and had to go back and forth at least twice a day. It was good exercise, except when it was cold and wet; it was not so pleasant. During our last year as sixth formers, we moved to the main building where all the eighteen-year-olds lived in one house. This was the only time we were separated by age.

Our classes were held in the main building. We had to go to chapel every day and twice on Sundays! Sunday was also our day for recreation, which included reading and knitting. It was also the day our clothing drawers were inspected for tidiness, with name tags showing. Nails and hair were also inspected.

Every Wednesday night there were concerts or art lectures in the main hall. So down we would go to the main hall and climb back up the hill at night. Attendance was mandatory for everyone. At the time I hated it, mainly because of the trip back and forth. But that's where I acquired my taste for classical music and ballet. On these evenings, we were allowed milk and biscuits after the performance. Our food was good overall but we had to eat everything that was served on our plate. As a result, when we got older, we were all obsessed with losing weight. I would come to the dining room late so I could sit as far as possible from the teacher at the table and somehow manage to get rid of some of my food.

As sixth-formers and eighteen-year-olds, we had one dance with the local boys' school. We were all (girls and boys) so terrified that we just stood in our corners, not knowing what to do. Later, I was told that all the Wycombe girls went wild in college, since they had no restrictions anymore.

My sister, the rebel, left school after taking her O-Levels, at the age of sixteen and returned to Iran. She had had enough.

The tragedy of it all was that I had no goals, passion or drive and went about my life in a robotic way. I was asked to stay and do my A-Levels. Since

I was not the rebellious type, I did what I was told and conformed to what was decided for me. I stayed and did my A-Levels. After that, Miss Fisher encouraged me to stay one more term to sit for the qualifying exam to go to Oxford or Cambridge University. She assured me that she could get me accepted into either. But there was no way I was staying one more term. I just couldn't bring myself to be at school for yet another year to do the Oxbridge exam.

Also, I did not have enough confidence in myself. I thought, 'Alright, you may be able to squeeze me in, but how am I going to stay in one of these prestigious Universities?' I really didn't think I could do it. Of course, my parents were not much of a guide. To be fair, they didn't know anything about all of this to advise me one way or the other. My father was a forward thinker and had very high hopes for me. He thought that one day I could be a lawyer, in the idealistic sense of law, not law as a profession. He knew that I didn't have the character of a lawyer but that I was smart and a good thinker.

I knew I didn't want to return to Iran, a country I didn't know, so I decided to delay it by going to Rome. I had no specific reason for this decision. When I was asked why Rome, unable to provide a viable reason, I said, 'I'm going to Rome to learn Italian'. So, my father asked a friend living in Rome if he knew of any other Iranian girls in Rome at that time. His friend knew a girl by the name of Ziba. So, off I went! My father's friend picked me up at the airport and took me to the student housing where Ziba lived. That's how I met Ziba, my close friend. We became inseparable. Six months later Ziba announced that her sister was joining her in Rome on her way to the American College of Switzerland. This is how I learned about the college. I called Guilda in Iran and told her:

> 'Guess what, we are going to college in Switzerland'.
> Her response was: 'Oh, okay I'll come!'

From that point, we created our own lives and our parents followed along. Since I had passed my A-Levels, I went into the college as a sophomore. Guilda started as a freshman and she stayed on one year longer than me.

When I think of those days at boarding school, there is a lot of sadness in me. Had I been English, it may have been a different experience. I have always felt homeless, regardless of where I have lived. I feel I don't belong and that I am not at home. I have never questioned my parents' actions or have any anger towards them. It isn't in my personality to carry a grudge or blame. My sister, however, does not feel the same way.

Travel to this day depresses me, especially trains and train stations. I always have anxiety before I travel. Even when going back to London, which I love. I have to get through the journey and then once I'm there I'm fine. The process is difficult, which is why it is always a challenge for me to make a decision to travel. It takes me back to the days of travelling to school by train, which was always depressing. From the time I was six until my move to America, I had not been in one place more than nine months. Even when we returned to Iran it was like going to a foreign country. I always felt an outsider. Which is why I have always felt a sense of homelessness. People ask me if I love Los Angeles and after all these years I tell them no because it doesn't feel like home. London, I loved and felt the closest to me, but last time I went it seemed like a foreign place to me since it had changed so much. The people and their attitudes have changed so it doesn't feel like home either. That's why I'm still searching. I don't know where I should go where I can say 'Oh my God this feels like home'.

I turned out to be very shy as a result of these experiences, sort of like a wounded animal. Before I went to boarding school my father called me '*jir jirak*' (cricket) because I never stopped talking. Soon after my arrival in England, I stopped. I lost my 'mother tongue'. Obviously, since I had left at the age of six, I never learned to read or write in Farsi. We were required to write to our parents weekly but only in English. The teachers could then read our letters to ensure we weren't saying anything negative about the school.

Within a year, I had forgotten any Farsi that I knew. I then developed a mental block for the language.

It was nice to go back home for the holidays although it wasn't specifically because it was home. It could have been anywhere. It was fun being with our friends going to tennis and swimming and out at night, when we were older. My parents never spent time with us, even though my mother was not working. Other than following my mother around if she needed to go to the tailor or something, we did not sit down to have a conversation on anything. Sometimes we would go as a family to friends' homes for dinner or to restaurants but that was it. Occasionally, my father would hire a private tutor to teach us Farsi but with little success. In spite of my talent for languages, I could never learn to read and write Farsi. I could speak French, English, Italian and German but not Farsi! This is one of my biggest regrets. Although I can speak the language now, I cannot read or write it.

I don't blame my parents because they thought they were doing their best. This was their best! Actually, I am very grateful to them. I blame myself and regret that I didn't take advantage of all the opportunities that were given to me. I feel I have let everyone down: my son, my father, myself and my siblings. I didn't take advantage of my talents.

In addition to her aptitude for languages, Shoreh is also an extremely creative artist with avant-garde ideas, but has not managed to achieve the success she has expected of herself. Presently she is working on a creative project that she hopes to make into a viable business venture.

My experiences at boarding school had a life-changing impact on me. I learned to be considerate of others. It was quite a shock when I came to this country (the U.S.) and found that quite the opposite was true. Here, each person was on their own. I would never change that learning for anything.

It was an amazing all-round education: culture, academics and discipline. It taught me to be independent. I have little patience for people who seek attention and are needy. I don't need attention. I am quite self-sufficient and satisfied to entertain myself. I don't even need passive entertainment like television or other forms of media. Although I feel homeless in that I don't call any country my own, I think I can be anywhere and find my own way. I'm not afraid of diversity in cultures. I've lived in a variety of countries, which allows me to adapt easily when I'm faced with the unknown. I'm still a loner, though I have fought this for many years. I get lonely, but the more I allow myself to be alone the easier it gets. In fact, I can be quite happy on my own where I can do things my way. After all, I have been on my own from the age of six and have become quite independent. Which is why when I'm with someone who is needy it really bothers me. I don't regret my boarding school experience and now that I reflect on my life and who I am today, I believe it is as a result of that period. I realize that it was a unique experience, which is impossible to duplicate today.

I really like the fact that I am different. For a long time, I wanted to be liked by everyone. I suppose deep down I thought that's why I was sent away and needed to be a pleaser. I believe I chose partners who wanted to be with me. That was good enough because I didn't know what it was I wanted. If they wanted me, then I must be special. I do like contradictions in life although I don't believe I'm an extremist.

My passion has always been for beauty and design, but I was ashamed. I never followed this passion because I didn't think I was good enough and could even get into the fashion industry. It would have been so easy at the time to work for one of the famous designer houses. The competition wasn't as steep as it is now. Had I followed my passion, perhaps my life would have taken a different turn.

After college, I was drawn back to Italy. This time I went to secretarial school and continued studying Italian. After a few months, my father told me to return to Iran. To keep me busy, he found me a job at a bank, Credit Suisse, which had recently opened in Tehran. Within a short period of time I had two men in my life. I married one of them and together we moved back to London.

I never went back to work after getting married. After my divorce from my first husband, I moved to the U.S. where I started working on my own designs. I have never really established roots in the U.S., believing that eventually I will move away again. I really don't feel like I belong anywhere.

Shoreh left Iran with her first husband who was posted with the Iranian Embassy in London after the revolution. After her divorce from her first husband she moved to Los Angeles with her son, spending much of her professional career as an interior designer, art collector and fashion designer. She lives in Beverly Hills, California, with her second husband and son.

11
PASSING IT ON

Soheila's story
Micklefield School, Seaford, Sussex (1968–1972)

Soheila and Soosan met at Micklefield in 1968 when Soheila, at the age of twelve, arrived at the school. Since then their lives have been intertwined in ways that they did not foresee. They live approximately ten minutes away from each other and often meet with their husbands. Soheila's two daughters and Soosan's children have also become friends. Their children now have their own friendships with their own young ones. Soosan's interview with Soheila took place at Soheila's home. After a few laughs and debate over having the interview in English or Farsi, Soheila proceeded to tell her story in English with occasional runaway Farsi phrases that seemed to enter the conversation naturally.

> My understanding is that the reason behind my being sent to England was that I had become a typical teenager. I attended pool parties with friends and fell behind in my studies. This impacted my grades at Hadaf[1] High School, where I had to retake a course in the summer. I think, perhaps, my mom thought that I wasn't doing what I was supposed to be doing and was getting side tracked. Being a single mom, she must have found managing a teenager a bit difficult. I was spending a lot of time with friends and though I knew I would do well at school, she didn't want to take the risk of my falling further behind.
>
> I lost my father when I was five and, according to Iranian law, my legal paternal uncle became my guardian. During this period, many families were sending their children abroad for education. Reluctantly, my uncle agreed with my mother to send me to a boarding school in England, but only because another cousin was already attending a school there. And so, arrangements were made for our departure.
>
> This was my first trip outside of Iran. I was travelling with my mother, so it didn't dawn on me that I was going to a strange country with a strange language. I was excited. I had a special haircut for the occasion and couldn't wait to go abroad. The idea of a boarding school had not registered with me nor, as far as I remember, was it ever explained to me. There was no discussion. My mother simply said, 'I am going to send you to school in England. Your cousin will be there'. And I thought – 'Great!'
>
> My recollection of those first days in London is connecting with another cousin and going shopping at High Street Kensington for a school uniform and all the other gear I needed. We then went on a train trip, which was fun. But it was also the first time I started to get worried. The fantasy of a foreign trip and shopping with my mother was over. Going to school in England became a reality and I started to get anxious. I remember arriving at the school, walking into the front foyer and meeting our headmistress, Mrs Wood, who greeted us kindly. I had learned a few words in English, but not enough to know what was going on. I just stood there. A single moment is very clear and salient to me. I turned around and they were no longer there; my mom and my cousin were gone. I will never forget that moment, thinking, where are my people? I can't remember what happened next.

Soheila tried to remember but appeared to be struggling to find adequate words with which to continue:

> It was ok, it was just that second which was a bit ... They went and I stayed!
>
> I was at the school until 1972 – so four years. I have mixed feelings about those years. I know that I could not bring myself to put my child through that experience. I say that recognizing, first, that I am not a single mother, second, I do not live in Iran any longer and third, I do not have the 'what if' questions that my mother appears to have had at the time. I think taking a child away from the family and putting her in a strange environment is traumatic. I could not do that; perhaps I am not as strong as my mother was.
>
> Having said that, I believe I owe who I am and where I am today to those four years. In that respect, I am grateful. It gave me a strong sense of confidence. I am totally comfortable with my English language where I would not have been otherwise. My fluency in English provides me the tool with which I am working today, so I appreciate that fact. I don't know who I would have become had I not been sent to boarding school. The experience was definitely positive in shaping my character.
>
> I also became a worldlier person, living in an environment where I had to fend for myself when I couldn't speak the language and had to deal with people who were foreign to me.
>
> Despite all the positives, I could not do the same to my child. It takes guts and courage and while I have a hard outer shell, on the inside I am too soft and unable to separate my children from the comfort of their home. So, maybe that is a credit to my mother and her strength.

Soheila's mother is affectionately called by her first name, Shokouh 'Joon', by Soheila herself and everyone else. She was and continues to be a strong, beautiful woman who tolerates no nonsense, just like her daughter. On a number of occasions, Soheila, along with Soosan and other Persian girls, spent half-term breaks and holidays at her mother's apartment in London. The girls were always excited to get away together and have her join them in their weekend follies.

> While I was at boarding school, Shokouh Joon lived in the London apartment for over a year. I would see her almost every two weeks and we spoke on the phone often. She stayed there to support me.
>
> Looking back to those years, there were lots of good and bad times. But I think I came away with my distinct character. I hate being a softy – except where my children are concerned – and boarding school is where I became strong. I gained confidence and I am happy to be who I am today. I learned social skills. I truly appreciate the British social etiquette, like their table manners! I laugh and joke about it and get teased by my children, but we were disciplined to eat properly, converse properly, sit properly and I have passed

some of these down to my children, even if these standards are difficult to maintain living in North America!

Of course, what I had learned in Iran was not very different so it was easy for me to adapt, but the standards were set much higher in England. In Iran eating with the family was the norm, behaving properly in the presence of others was important. The rules were the same but they were stricter and totally enforced in England. Boarding school provided quality education and strict discipline, but a generally happy environment.

One of my experiences relates to living in a residence hall outside of the main school building. It must have been after the first night. One morning, a group of girls, including Cynthia, my assigned mentor who was also in charge of our home class, went to the main building. I was sitting in the classroom when the matron walked in and said something to Cynthia. Subsequently, I was called out of the class. I was curious as to what I had done. The matron took me back to the house because I had not made my bed. I remember thinking this is strange! Do they really expect me to make my own bed?

These are the kinds of experiences that have made me resilient. I had never made my own bed before; I was never asked to. I also remember taking a bath filled with only a couple of inches of water. It was really awkward. There were no showers and I was expected to clean and dry everything when I finished and before my time was up.

I learned a great deal from the other girls, especially Cynthia. She was from Malaysia. She would talk and talk about her interests and her feelings. She was a great support to me and we continue to remain very close friends. Of course, there were also the other Persian girls with whom I became friends. It was like I wanted to grab something or someone I could relate to, so getting together with them was important to me. I was determined to make it work. I value the friendships I have made, specifically with all the Persian girls. We have a connection that is unique and meaningful. They give me something precious every time we are together.

I missed my friends in Iran and wrote letters to them often but I did not miss my old school. The prospect of being back in Iran at the time was not appealing. There was an economic boom because of oil and we lived in the high society, but I was young and not involved in all that. I was eager to return home in the summer to see my family, but I never wished I hadn't left. Once I learned to speak English, understood and related to people, I began to have fun. I enjoyed being there. The education exposed me to the English language and literature. I had the best elocution teacher.

Of course, going back to Iran in the summer was the highlight of the year, although throughout the year I had my mother living in London.

I had a few experiences with some girls where I felt that I was being bullied. It was not bullying as we understand it today. For instance, I was sharing a room with another girl who had blond hair. One day, I found my hairbrush full of blond hair and knew she had used it (Soheila has black curly hair). I didn't know how to tell her not to use my hairbrush but fought back with my broken English anyway. We had a full-out fight about this, probably with sign language! I was young and inexperienced, but having had those experiences at such a young age taught me to stand up for myself. I learned to stay emotionally detached from things that may hurt me and not to have deep connections.

Every evening, before we walked back to our House, we had an hour or so to spend by ourselves. I spent those hours in the library pulling out words from the dictionary. There was a younger Persian girl who spoke fluent English. I would ask her quietly to read the words out for me so that I could get the pronunciation correct.

Despite my foolish teenage behaviour at school in Iran, I was always academically focused and my grades were excellent. In England, I took subjects like biology, physics, chemistry and maths. My friend Delbar often reminded me that I couldn't manage these difficult subjects simultaneously, but I did not listen. I wanted to challenge myself and prove that I could. Like all the other Persian girls, I knew I was there to learn English, study well and go to university. That was the predetermined route for most of us. My goal was to become a brain surgeon and that is why I took those subjects, but I later realized I wasn't as good as I believed to be in subjects like biology or physics but I was much better at maths.

By the time I was ready for university, I wanted to become a chartered accountant. Although I was accepted at the university, I completed a HND (Higher National Diploma) and became a chartered accountant. I returned to Iran after my marriage in England and joined my husband in managing his business.

Soheila and her family live in Toronto. She and her husband collaborate on a number of business initiatives in Canada and Iran, often travelling between the two countries. Trained as an accountant in England, she works tirelessly in Canada as an official translator and personal representative within the Canadian legal system. She facilitates document presentations and legal arguments on behalf of Iranian and Afghani residents and refugees. She is the Founder and President of the Association of Professional Language Interpreters. The goal of the organization is to support and advocate for interpreters, professionalize the interpretation industry and prevent incidents of misconduct and misinterpretation among service users and providers.

Note

1   Hadaf educational group was a pioneering private complex founded in Iran in 1949. With the objective of providing high-quality education from elementary to high school, it was comparable to American preparatory schools. The overwhelming majority of Hadaf graduates continued their higher education in leading Western universities.

SUMMARY

The stories of Soosan, Shoreh and Soheila exemplify the behaviours that have now become habitual, resisting any expression of intense emotions or admission of vulnerabilities to protect themselves from hurt. Ultimately, they left their childhood years behind with friendships that served as pillars of support, without which their loneliness would have been hard to endure. Their deep sense of loyalty, love and camaraderie for their boarding school friends remains as strong and deep rooted as they once were even as they cautiously and selectively form new ones. They do so, occasionally doubtful, like many of the other girls, wondering what their lives would have been like had they reacted differently to their boarding school experience.

Soosan's story portrays the metal trunk as an important metaphor for the life she led. It accompanied her from dorm to dorm, packing and unpacking over the years in and outside of boarding school. Accustomed to and thrilled by change, in the years to come she creates her own tune while at the same time selflessly caring for those she loves, perhaps still striving to be 'special'. Living a secure contented life filled with accomplishments, she has learned not to look back or wonder what life could have been, but to look forward grounded in the trust and space for independence that was bestowed on her at an early age.

After eleven years of boarding school experience, Shoreh's feelings of homelessness and loss of voice casts a shadow on her life as she continues to wonder what could have been. Her common feelings of loneliness, abandonment and ultimately fear of vulnerability and lack of confidence strongly influenced who she became as an adult. She strives to express her passion and creativity through her designs and sense of style believing that her creative talents were stifled with the rules, regulations and structures that were imposed on her. She conveys her individuality in her particular and nuanced eating habits which culminated in her book, *Camelot's Kitchen*, but ultimately declares comfort in her loneliness.

In the end, Soheila, proud of all that has been and grateful for the privilege of experiencing boarding school, attributes much of who she is today to her early exposure to British discipline, norms and values. She fought bullying with broken English and learned to stand up for herself. Today, she invests her energy into defending refugees in the Canadian courts of law. Her sense of integrity and desire for ethical professional practices are combined with her commitment to the Persian culture as she instils those values in her children and grandchildren.

PART IV
Lives we shared

It's wise for all of us to keep in mind that we're in process, and to keep on our traveling shoes.

Maya Angelou[1]

Boarding or residential schools, whether preparing students for prestigious colleges, assimilating aboriginal Canadians into mainstream society or enabling African Americans to gain trade skills, have long been the subject of social and psychological debate in Western society. In Britain, where boarding schools have been a permanent and evolving feature of the education system, they mainly serve as training grounds for the children of affluent English families living in England or abroad. To non-English privileged families, who aspire to have their children educated in British ways, these schools symbolize 'Englishness' and have been growing in popularity.

In contrast to this growing popularity, research on the educational outcome or the psychological impact on children and, in particular, non-English children who spend their adolescent years in such schools, has been limited and contentious.

In perhaps the largest study of boarding schools across a representative sample of hundreds of schools in Australia, North America and U.K., Martin, Papworth, Ginns and Liem (2014)[2] concluded that there is a predominant parity between boarding and day students on factors such as motivation, engagement and psychological well-being. Defining boarding school as a controlled, residential educational program, Bass (2014)[3] argued that the unique, structured environment of boarding school has a positive impact on a student's academic experience in part because it shelters students who come from unsupportive homes from negative outside influences. Elias (2012)[4] and colleagues determined that some ex-boarders have fared well while others have suffered complex mental and emotional challenges. Schavarien (2004)[5] considered sending young children to boarding school a particularly British form of child abuse. Duffell[6] (2012) and Schaverien (2011) extensively explored ex-boarder stories of trauma and mental health challenges. They reported the negative effects from boarding school experiences and/or ambivalence (positive and negative) by former students about their past school attendance.

In 2011, Schaverien[7] coined the term 'boarding school syndrome' in a paper in *The British Journal of Psychiatry*, arguing that boarding schools 'can cause profound developmental damage'. In response Duffel (2012) identified what he calls the 'Strategic Survival Personality' of former boarders. Providing a clinical perspective, he stated that a child develops emotional strategies to survive the ordeal of being sent away from home, having to rapidly become 'independent', 'grown up' and 'self-sufficient'. Such strategies split off and 'hide' the vulnerable and dependent parts of a child, who on the surface appears competent, successful and independent. Duffel also divided 'survivors' of boarding schools into three categories. First, the 'compliers', live in denial of their experience yet find themselves in trouble when their survival strategy is threatened through a work or relationship crisis. Second, the 'rebels', with their anti-authoritarian stance, refuse to live up to their potential. They become 'engaging but infuriating' individuals with a need to be challenged and told to 'stop surviving and start living'. And finally, there are the 'casualties' who 'have barely survived'. They seem unable to build a successful survival personality and continue to remain at the bottom of the pile. In response to these findings, numerous support groups have emerged and websites such as www.boardingschoolsurvivors.co.uk and www.boardingrecovery.com offer therapeutic workshops for 'survivors' of boarding school in an attempt to enable them to build a normal life.

Critics of boarding school education contend that the boarding school tradition has gone unchallenged for too long. Over the years, however, the austere schools of the past, á la Dickens' *Nicholas Nickleby*, have transformed themselves to meet modern standards by paying attention to the needs of individual students. In fact, websites promoting the British boarding school education attribute the continuous success of such schools to their efforts in providing a combination of low student-to-staff ratios, investment in facilities, as well as maintaining the traditions and ethos that address the needs of students as individuals. In short, the schools now claim to do far more than simply prepare pupils to do well on examinations; that the 'tradition and ethos' that has continued throughout the ages, is focused on developing the whole person, instilling self-belief and self-confidence and, more importantly, developing effective social skills by having children live in a multi-age, multicultural community. At the same time, today's informed parents make their choice of schools based on league tables and rankings rather than word of mouth. As a result, these schools continue to prosper in a competitive environment while they strive to develop personal and interpersonal qualities such as kindness, tolerance and responsibility.

Exploring the long-term psychological effects of a boarding school education has been the central theme of this book. Specifically, we have attempted to explore the embodied experiences of 'little rich Persian girls', who crossed cultures in order to acquire what our parents believed to be the best education possible.

Brown and Gilligan[8] (1993) mark adolescence as a watershed moment in women's psychological development. We thought that our adolescent experiences as girls, given our privileged upbringing, might distinguish us from individuals, particularly women, of different cultural and societal groups. In the absence of sufficient empirical studies or theoretical frameworks regarding boarding school experiences of privileged students, we approached our interpretation of stories informed by multidisciplinary perspectives from developmental, social and cross-cultural psychology. Our goal has not been to 'problematize' boarding school education nor to prescribe solutions, but rather to further our collective understanding of the embedded and emergent experiences of women within the context of the worlds they live in.

From a sociocultural perspective, we understand that some environments may evoke different motivational reactions and that specific school cultures also shaped the individual student's belief system (Martin, Papworth, Ginns & Malmberg 2016).[9] So, we rely on the stories themselves to shed light on why the boarding school education system was selected, the different learning and social activities we engaged in and the coping strategies that we used for 'survival'. They present a collage of the elaborate system of rules and regulations, which accounted for and controlled every moment of our time. Our constructed narratives speak to the uniqueness of the individuals behaviour, the shaping of character, beliefs, values and skills, and how each of us interpreted our lived boarding school experience. We explore the salient pattern of these activities and give meaning to the interpersonal relationships that have had a direct impact on our psychological development. We highlight the Persian and British cross-cultural challenges we encountered as children and the impact of this cultural dichotomy on our lives as adults.

In many instances, the stories are the manifestation of a conflicted relationship with parents and the continued effort to reconcile contradicting cultural values. Parents and parenting style are central to a young person's development as evident in Bowlby's (1969) psychological attachment theory.[10] This theory states that perceived accessibility to primary caretakers influences children's internal workings towards one of security, anxiety and ambivalence or avoidance. Individuals with a secure attachment style, trust others and consider themselves worthy of love while those with anxious and ambivalent attachment develop a high need for dependence. Their desire for closeness with others together with their fear of rejection often triggers anger when they find those significant others inaccessible. The avoidant style finds its roots in a pattern of rejections and results in negative view of others in contrast to an inflated positive view of self. According to Latham and Heslin (2003)[11] these attachment styles are shaped by a child's belief that (a) she is worthy of love and (b) that she can depend on significant others to be accessible. Bowlby considers the attachment bond to be universal, but little is known about the impact of culture on or the nature of this attachment. There are cultural differences in the emphasis that is placed on how children relate to parents and the expectations that parents place on their children. For example, positive parenting defined by a collective Persian culture and associated with authoritarian parental behaviour that encourages dependency, is quite different from positive parenting understood within an individualistic British culture that encourages autonomy and independence.

Being away from home at a young age means being deprived of the most important influence and intimate care, at times resulting in negative effects as evident in the stories of Shoreh (Chapter 10) where she expresses feelings of homelessness into adulthood or Dory's (Chapter 5) consistent 'hatred' of her parents and ongoing fear of vulnerability. At the same time, it would appear that the distance from home at a young age offered the opportunity for attachment with siblings, peers and other adults, who positively influenced the girls in terms of resilience, a sense of independence and the ability to cope with changing home and social environment. Carlson and Harwood (2003)[12] showed that controlling care giving, characterized by valuing well-behaved children, results in a secure attachment. Chao and Tseng (2002)[13] found that such parenting was associated with subsequent academic success and socio-emotional wellbeing. The boarding school system with its authoritarian British educators and administrators and the attachment formed with them in part reinforced the Persian parents' expectations for respectful and appropriate social behaviour. This may explain the general source of security and confidence in Soheila (Chapter 11) or Roxane's (Chapter 8) sociability and her proclaimed love of institutions. Furthermore, the attachment formed with peers and siblings played a significant role in the everyday lives of the 'Persian girls'. While at school, we formed strong bonds of friendship with influence on each other extending well beyond our adolescence into adult years.

Our stories unfold experiences across six different boarding schools (Charters Towers, Micklefield, Grove School, Moira House, Lowther College and Hargrove Abbey). Roya's (Chapter 1) story portrays a landscape of life at Charter Towers that draws on similarities with all other schools in terms of the school structure, daily routines, vacation practices and interactions with peers and teachers. In particular, her story reflects the close enduring friendships with her peers mirrored in those of Soosan (Chapter 4) and her school mates and ones that others like Fereshteh (Chapter 2) aspired to and yearned for. While at school, we studied, played, travelled and lived together. The emotional support that we provided for each other filled a void that was deepened by strict school rules and harsh practices of the authority figures, namely, matrons and house mistresses. At Charters Towers, we (Shirley, Azy, Roxane and Roya) became inseparable best friends forming the core of an intimate group, supporting each other during good and bad times and developing an unbreakable bond. The friendship of this tight group extended to bonding with the rest of the Persian girls at school during the Sunday religious gathering when other students were in church.

At Micklefield, we (Soheila, Sheila and Soosan) formed a group that included other Persian girls, spending our time together at school and during holidays. Among our most memorable time at Micklefield was when, away from the watchful eyes of authority figures, we gathered to listen to Sheila play the piano in a secluded music room. Emotionally inspired by her music and passionate rendering of Persian songs, we shared stories and confided in each other. At the time, like the girls from Charters Towers and most other adolescent girls, we revelled in our temporary refuge of a small group of friends who could understand and empathize with our plight. In fact, we gathered together with other Persian girls on every possible occasion regardless of our age difference or religious beliefs. Within this cherished microcosm, we spoke our native Farsi language and exposed the nostalgia we felt but had learned to keep hidden as we kept moving forward. We shared adolescent dreams without fear of judgment and experienced the bonds of friendship in ways that would not have been possible with anyone other than a 'Persian' girl. Unknowingly and perhaps intuitively, we developed attachments that helped us survive our feelings of loss and abandonment, forming close relationships with those with whom we identified, without fear of vulnerability or dependence. These intimate friendships allowed us to express collective and supportive behaviours that we had been used to back at home in Iran.

Schaverien (2011) has identified the inability to express or interpret emotion, generalized depression and problems with intimacy, as symptoms among the 'ex-boarders' she has counselled. 'They get on with the job and so on,' says Schaverien, 'but they never talk about their feelings'. The syndrome is not news to us or to the hordes of ex-boarders who gather online in solidarity and campaign against 'early boarding', particularly for children aged between seven and thirteen. Unlike other adolescent girls who live with their families, we had no parent to run to, complain to or seek help from when we faced trouble. We only had each other. Whether it was hiding in a piano room to listen to music, going to the tuck shop wearing our best clothes or escaping to London for a shopping spree, we trusted each other and divulged our secrets knowing that we were for the moment safe. We felt free when we were among our own people. This feeling of trust and safety has carried us into our relationships with each other to the present, relationships that have survived our turbulent post-revolution experiences. However, it was only after reviewing Sheila's story (Chapter 7) that we questioned whether our relationships with each other, strong and sustainable as they were, had been enough.

Sheila's story highlighted the very essence of the unique emotional connections we needed as children to become whole. For Sheila, music was more than an escape or the chance for moments of carefree laughter with compatriots. This was how she accessed her emotions and how she connected with the world within and around her. She found meaning through her music long before she had any meaningful relationship with others, until she met her musically talented husband. While we acknowledge that it was in part our bonding with each other that sustained us then, we are aware of the unique emotional connection with 'other' that evaded us. Many of us did not experience the dramas and joys of relationships with the opposite sex before we were married, which perhaps explains why so many of our marriages failed. Of the eleven girls featured in this book, only Roya and Soheila have remained married to the same man. Although the divorce rate is high in the general population too, it seems higher than average in this group. Perhaps this is because we believed that we could make it on our own.

Closer to our hearts, however, was our attachment to our siblings who had made the journey before us, together with us or sometimes a few years after. This feeling was particularly strong with our older sisters who were the pioneers and whose absence from home was felt by those of us left behind, we younger sisters. Their simple presence in England, whether at the same school or another, gave us comfort and kept us secure. Soosan (Chapter 4) looked forward to spending holidays with her older sister Sudi, who was sent two years earlier to Grove School in Surrey. Roya (Chapter 1) and her older sister Vida, both went to Charter Towers school one year apart. Though they have different memories of their experiences, they supported each other through thick and thin. Azy (Chapter 3) was an older sister who became a mother figure to her younger sister, Heidi, and her brother a few years later. Dory (Chapter 5), too, supported her younger siblings through challenging experiences. Saghi's (Chapter 9) older step-brother and sister had left boarding school by the time Saghi arrived, but the family tradition of attending boarding school eased the way for her. Shirley (Chapter 6) was sent directly to her older married sister Flora, who assumed her guardianship. Shoreh (Chapter 10) and her sister, Guilda, left home together at the ages of six and seven to live with their guardian, Mrs Fox. Finally, Roxane (Chapter 8) was joined by her younger brother and became responsible for taking care of him.

We also developed personal relationships with other women, namely our teachers, guardian or the adults who took care of us during our holidays. We learned to depend on them for guidance and direction. In the absence of our parents, these individuals were the adults with whom we shared our lives. Our narrative of these women is based, for the most part, on the memories of how we saw them when we were young girls. They played a significant role in the shaping of our character during our adolescent years. These women soon became our role models as wives, mothers and professionals. In our stories, we remember the charismatic Mrs Peck, the disciplinarian Miss McGarry, the caring Mrs Thomson and the protective Mrs Eaton; the strong women who left a footprint on our lives.

Among the most remembered is Miss McGarry, the headmistress at Charters Towers. She is an ever present figure of authority for Roya, Shirley, Roxane and Azy. Their memories of her vary but are most vividly recalled in Roya's (Chapter 1) story. She describes Miss McGarry as:

> a tall, good-looking, stout, middle-aged woman, always impeccably dressed in her colourful raw silk suits. She was always perfectly groomed and, despite her thick glasses, was an attractive woman. Her signature Givenchy perfume trailed her as a warning of her arrival or that she was in the vicinity. She had a very stern look and rarely smiled. There was an aura about her that instilled fear in all of us. Just her presence made me shudder with apprehension wondering if I was giving her cause to reprimand me in any way, even if she was just passing by.

Miss McGarry was a highly cultured and educated art historian who was passionate about the subject. She aimed to instil this same passion and education in her students. When it came to guardians, Mrs Peck's strong character speaks for itself in the story 'Our Guardian Mrs Peck' (Appendix I). Her stylishly furnished home in Kew Gardens was the place we looked forward to visiting before or after going home to Iran. Roxane (Chapter 8) remembers a family friend, Mrs Eaton, who owned a bed and breakfast in London, as her 'go-to' person in times of need and the hotel, her home away from home.

Ironically, our parents had little or no awareness of the existence of these other women, let alone their influence on our lives. Living among these families, we learned to live an English life and be a member of a family, albeit not our own. In the absence of immediate and tangible maternal love, we looked to friends, siblings, educators and guardians who formally or informally seemed to have assumed responsibility for our physical and perhaps psychological wellbeing. Over the years, within the context of a boarding school and the British homes we lived in, we made every effort to learn the British culture, its history, traditions, norms and values and to behave accordingly. But our emerging 'Englishness' was inseparable from our sense of identity and who we were as 'Persian' girls. French (2006)[14] explains that early child–parent contact encourages internalization of cultural values. Our adolescent experiences, entrenched in the contrasting British culture, magnified our desire to hold on to our Persian identity, an identity that we had taken for granted in our childhood. In the end, whether we acculturated or considered ourselves Saghi or Sally (Chapter 9), our fundamental desire for belonging according to Maslow (1970)[15] constituted an important aspect of our self-concept and our identity as 'Persian Girls'.

Identities are shaped by life experiences. Bridging the gap between individual agency and social and cultural influences, it is, according to Ybema (2009)[16] and colleagues, the result of a 'dynamic interplay between internal strivings and external prescriptions, between self-presentation and labelling by others, between achievement and ascription and between regulation and resistance' (p. 301). Our identity construction, as evident by our narratives, is in part an outcome of the particular time period we spent at a boarding school. Our narratives, based on our conscious and unconscious recollection, account for events that have shaped our sense of self, including our social and cultural identity.

Little is known about the development of the acculturation process. However, the stories we have shared in this book reveal the forming of our bicultural identities. We lived our lives at boarding school, and later as adults in the West, based on our personal disposition and unique character traits such as independence, vulnerability, agreeableness, determination and confidence. Living in an unfamiliar culture can be daunting for an adult, but for most of us as young girls, the idea of doing so was filled with mystery, a sense of excitement together with a fear of the unknown. How each of us responded, embraced the thrill or feared abandonment, was moderated by who we were as young girls and how we took control of our own lives later as mature women. Our personality traits not only influenced the nature of our relationship with our parents and caregivers, they also affected how we conformed to expected social behaviours and whether we accepted or adapted to cultural differences and the demands imposed on us. Berry (2005)[17] asserts that acculturation is inevitable when one migrates to live in another culture because it results in experiences that impact an individual's affect, behaviour and cognition. Whether we knew how to speak English or we had lived outside Iran prior to our placement in boarding school, the cultural differences between Iran and England were bound to influence our behaviour, let alone how those behaviours were perceived by others at home or in England.

As children, most of us quickly adjusted to our new way of life in an effort to bridge the gap between our new found liberating individualism in England and the restrictive communitarianism we were expected to adhere to when in Iran. At boarding school, we were asked to be mature, taught to be independent, to make difficult personal choices and to be responsible for the consequences of our own behaviour. As young girls, we learned to take care of ourselves and as we grew up, we began to trust our own judgment of right and wrong. Our parents seemed to trust us when we were away with shopping assignments and responsibility for our finances. They showed confidence that we could manage our commute across the continent to get to our holiday destination, whether in Europe or back home in Iran. As a result, every summer we returned to our homes with the expectation of living in a collectivist culture with our newly gained sense of Western individualism. But living in Iran was different. There, we returned to being the young girl who was to behave according to expectations and norms of the Iranian culture and those of our respective families. We had to consider the impact of our behaviour on our parents' reputation and that of our broader family. What an aunt or an uncle, neighbour or client thought became important again. After all, we had been sent to boarding school to 'become who our parents wished us to become!'

There are those of us who believe that managing the tension between our two cultures affected our character development and suppressed who we were 'meant' to be. Both Saghi (Chapter 9) and Dory (Chapter 5) reveal a sense of suffocation of their true identity in telling their stories. According to Berry (2006),[18] a person's orientation style to acculturation varies in four different ways: integration (holding positive orientation to both cultures), assimilation (adaptation to a new culture), separation (holding on to heritage culture and minimizing adoption of the new culture) and marginalization (low interest in maintaining or adopting to either culture). The modal orientation, integration, is deemed vital for psychological well-being and development of a bicultural identity. In this context, it is noteworthy that despite our adolescent experiences, the contradictions of cultural values between Iran and England and our struggle to identify as 'Saghi or Sally', we learned to navigate between cultures in ways that ultimately allowed us to be at once true to our roots and to our upbringing in the British culture. It seems that the very experience of going back and forth to Iran during those summer holidays, or visiting European countries with or without our parents, served as a strong motivating factor for us to develop a bicultural identity. At the same time, there is evidence of loss, feelings of abandonment, relational conflicts and a continuing struggle for voice as we try to balance our feelings and thoughts with the expectation of, and in relationship to others, in particular our parents.

Dealing with ambivalence towards parents, who are simultaneously loved and hated by their adolescent child, is indeed not unique to Persian girls sent away from home. 'There is not a parent on earth who hasn't occasionally hated their child. There's not a child who hasn't sometimes hated a parent, and that's just how it is' (Duffell, 2000).[19] In many instances, however, our stories reveal a persistent conflicted relationship with our parents, who we hold responsible for a major decision that, without doubt, impacted our lives. The answers to our questions as to why we were sent away eluded us but sometimes manifested themselves in our reactions such as running away, depression, crying and solitude, followed by years of therapy and ultimately a distant relationship with parents, struggles with intimacy and divorce from a loved one. The willingness to share our stories implies a personal need to express deeply embedded conflicting feelings of sadness and abandonment combined with hope and optimism. We had left behind the lives we knew; our country, language, families and friends, to arrive with excitement in a new land of unknowns. Cultural values and family expectations followed us to England to ensure that we delivered on our parents' expectations. These values gave us hope and kept us grounded. And yet once alone in England, we encountered a new reality. Regardless of our age, we were left alone, expected to act as a grown up, to put up and deal with whatever was thrown at us and most importantly to take control of our own lives. As children, we trusted the decisions of our fathers and strived to please them despite our yearning for their presence. Today, we look back, no longer children thrilled by the idea of adventure or freedom from the rules of our parents, and attempt to reconcile conflicting feelings about the decision to be sent away. We attempt to justify our parents' reasons for separating us from our families, acknowledging that they were as Winnicott (1962)[20] indicates 'good enough' parents. We claim not to be perfect parents ourselves and therefore do not hold them to that standard either. In our search for answers, we continue to look deeply into our own story and the story of others who shared our experience.

Erikson (1968)[21] believes that adolescence is the developmental stage when one begins to search for meaning and one's life purpose. In retrospect, whether we wore our skirts shorter than the regulation, spoke Farsi as opposed to English, walked around barefoot against the rules or snuck out of the school at odd hours for a glance of freedom in town, we were simply finding meaning and forming an identity that was to define our later lives. While at school, a few of us laid low and remained invisible in the crowd even as we refused to conform to social and cultural norms. Others among us, such as Shirley (Chapter 6) and Azy (Chapter 3), experiencing highly restrictive forms of control, rebelled, our vulnerability kept intact, determined to access our unique personal resources to find a voice of our own. Naturally, with severe British discipline, there was no shortage of adult authoritative supervision and reprimands. We were told consistently to 'pull our socks up' sometimes, as in the case of Shirley, we would take it literally! She was the youngest child of four with a large age gap between her and her siblings.

She was 'trouble' by her own admission and believed that her father adored, trusted and respected her. This appears to have given rise to a twelve-year-old girl with remarkable self-confidence and a strong sense of security. Unlike many of the other girls, Shirley had found her 'voice' (literally as well as figuratively) early in life, even in expressing her opinion on the decision to go to boarding school.

By all accounts, the British boarding school was designed not only to educate us in English literature, art, history and philosophy, but it was also designed to build our character, providing us with a unique educational and social experience. We were indeed provided a first-rate education. But, we cannot recollect any form of guidance towards a particular profession or preparation for a life that promised achievement. In fact, even if any of us had any aspiration of a profession, as in Roya's dream to become a doctor, it was nipped in the bud in favour of compliance with the so-called 'traditional role' of a 1960s woman. Shoreh's (Chapter 10) dissatisfaction with her accomplishments and feelings that she was not able to maximize the potential of her creativity are a consistent reflection of a lasting craving for approval. The exception is Roxane (Chapter 8) who, bribed by her father to stay on at school for her A-Levels, and was accepted to both Harvard and Oxford. She pursued her studies at Harvard, despite her father's disapproval of her travelling to the U.S., and followed a life of self-inflicted pressure for performance and high achievement.

At the time, the Micklefield school motto of 'To Love and Serve', was not defined for us in terms of a career. We were educated in the British way and learned about Western culture and civilization. We were trained to speak well with clear diction, dress appropriately for different occasions and behave in a manner acceptable for women of the day. The implicit goal on the part of our parents and educators was to prepare us for finding a 'good' husband and, ultimately, becoming a good wife and mother. As such, our primary concern as teenagers was to meet school and family obligations, regardless of the challenges we faced or the dreams we may have had. The British values we were introduced to were based on the culture of the school and those of the adults who educated us. Our educators were primarily single, widowed or divorced women (and a few men) who had entered the workforce after the Second World War. They emphasized inner virtue rather than external charm. They had grown up in a 'culture of character' when duty, hard work, morals, manners and integrity were more important than today's 'culture of personality' defined by charisma, attractiveness and personal magnetism. They stressed these values to us.

Growing up among culturally different people today is the norm. We were exposed to this notion early in life. At school, we were taught to respect others' culture, space and their rights to do as they pleased; to allow people to be who they were. 'International Day' was taken very seriously and celebrated every year. All girls were expected to participate in this festive event. At Charters Towers, each country had a station and the girls wore their ethnic clothes, performed traditional dances or shared memorabilia from their home countries. At the closing ceremony, the eldest girl from each country would light a candle representing their country. In our innocence, we found the prejudices of our own family members back home baffling, whether it was Shirley's sister's aversion to a black roommate (Chapter 6) or Soosan's family's overwhelming adoration of her white English friend, Barbara, on her visit to Iran (Chapter 4). Iranians, much like other cultures, have many biases and prejudices around different ethnic backgrounds. Our exposure to other traditions in boarding school, along with day-to-day living with diverse individuals, cultivated an openness to and acceptance of these differences. As members of an ethnic group, we recognized the issues facing students from other cultures, identified with them and were willing to learn about them and at the same time educated them about our own culture. We experienced multiculturalism at school and our ability to identify with both the British and the Persian cultures later served us well when many of us settled for a life in the West.

Today, we have a newfound appreciation for our experiences in a boarding school. At the end of the day, we acquired skills, knowledge and abilities that may not have been possible otherwise. Soheila (Chapter 11), whose story is about ultimate gratitude, resilience and, more importantly, personal agency derived from the desire to exert control over her own life, voices this claim the loudest. The Oxford English Dictionary describes a resilient person as one who is able to return to patterns of behaviour prior to the time of stress stating that 'under adversity, a (resilient) individual can bend ... yet subsequently recover'. We collectively attribute our sense of independence, resilience, as well as our worldliness to what we learned at boarding school but perhaps our early childhood experiences in a warm, supportive family environment in Iran has as much to do with who we are today. Our bicultural identity and the ability to cope with and/or adapt to changing social environments and effectively integrate and communicate with people of all cultures, have contributed positively to the lives we have lived in the West.

Now, as parents and grandparents, we increasingly recognize that the past consistently influences and determines our present actions. While we are by no means free of the insidious conditioning of our adolescent years, we move forward towards the next cycle of our lives with a clearer understanding of the lives we experienced and the reasons we made our decisions. In some ways, we have all learned to give meaning to the Micklefield School logo of 'To Love and Serve'. Our own migration experiences have allowed us, not only to juggle cultures, but to understand, share and empathize with people from other cultures. We have become of age and taken steps to give back to those in need of care or seeking support. Just as our educators had learned from their experience, following our disrupted lives after the Iranian Revolution in 1979, we too have turned to 'making a difference in the world', each in our own way:

Fereshteh (Chapter 2) engages the five cosmic elements (wood, fire, metal, water and earth) to care for her patients by relieving their pain as an acupuncturist.

Azy (Chapter 3) founded the Iranian Scholarship Foundation in 2000. Since then it has provided scholarships and funds for the college education of hundreds of students of Iranian descent in the U.S., enabling them to turn their educational dreams into reality. The funds are available to those who are financially disadvantaged but who demonstrate exceptional academic promise and dedication to community service.

Dory (Chapter 5) has a thriving coaching practice, supporting her clients to fulfil their life purpose as they live their lives according to their values. She has also been assisting her sister in the growth and development of the OMID (Hope) Foundation since 2004.

Shirley (Chapter 6) founded Magic of Persia in 2004 to promote the culture and arts of her beloved Iran. The foundation promotes and introduces upcoming Iranian artists to a worldwide audience through fundraising and other promotional events.

Sheila (Chapter 7) works tirelessly along with her husband, sharing her love of music and inspiring children through her unique method of teaching music as a language system of emotional expression. She integrates Western and Eastern music to satisfy her love of Persian classical music.

Roxane's (Chapter 8) love of aesthetics brought her to her leadership role as the director of Middle Eastern Art at Sotheby's. After graduating from Harvard and obtaining her PhD from Oxford, she joined Sotheby's in 2006. She has responsibility implementing the company's strategy in the Middle East and North Africa.

Saghi's (Chapter 9) abundant energy is devoted to motherhood as she supports her family especially her adolescent son through his last years of school.

Shoreh (Chapter 10) has followed her passion for creativity and design. She has created a clothing line for Middle Eastern women, including a new line of fashionable hats, thus enhancing the femininity of the Hijab attire.

Soheila (Chapter 11) is the founder of the Association of Professional Interpreters. This organization supports and advocates integrity and professionalism among interpreters who work with refugees from Iran and Afghanistan in the Canadian legal system.

We, the authors, work as life and leadership coaches, enabling others' discovery of their own paths through their own narratives, while we continue to develop ourselves:

Roya, (Chapter 1) after many years in the corporate world and graduate degrees in business and health services administration, followed her passion first as a health and fitness coach and then a certified life and executive coach. She supports her clients in living a balanced life, as they work to attain their personal and professional goals.

Soosan (Chapter 4), currently a York University professor in Toronto and a former JP Morgan human resources executive, is teaching young adults and coaching executives, developing cross-cultural leaders, one leader at a time.

Dory summarized our current lives well in saying:

'Perhaps the force drawing us to give back to our communities and in particular to bridge the Eastern and Western cultures, has been as a result of the pain we felt in our own lives, allowing us space for compassion for the "discarded, displaced or disconnected from society"'.

In our continued pursuit of discovering who we are and understanding of our self, our cognitive coping strategies and emotional challenges, we have found truth in Gandhi's words:

'The best way to find yourself is to lose yourself in the service of others'.

Notes

1 Gillespie, M. A., Butler, R. J. and Long, R. A. (2008), *Maya Angelou: A Glorious Celebration*, Doubleday, New York.
2 Martin, A. J., Papworth, B., Ginns, P. and Liem, G. A. D. (2014), Boarding school, academic motivation and engagement, and psychological well-being: A large-scale investigation, *American Educational Research Journal*, 51(5), 1007–1049.
3 Bass, L. R. (2014), Boarding schools and capital benefits: Implications for urban school reform, *The Journal of Educational Research*, 107(1), 16–35.
4 Elias, B., Mignone, J., Hall, M., Hong, S. P., Hart, L. and Sareen, J. (2012), Trauma and suicide behaviour histories among a Canadian indigenous population: An empirical exploration of the potential role of Canada's residential school system, *Social Science & Medicine*, 74(10), 1560–1569.
5 Schaverien, J. (2004), Boarding school: The trauma of the 'privileged' child, *Journal of Analytical Psychology*, Wiley Online Library.
6 Duffell, N. (2012), Response to Elizabeth Standish's Review of Joy Schaverien's (2011) Article 'Boarding school syndrome: Broken attachments a hidden trauma'. *British Journal of Psychotherapy*, 28(1), 126–128.
7 Schaverien, J. (2011), Boarding school syndrome: Broken attachments a hidden trauma. *British Journal of Psychotherapy*, 27(2), 138–155.
8 Brown, L. M. and Gilligan, C. (1993), Meeting at the crossroads: Women's psychology and girls' development, *Feminism & Psychology*, 3(1), 11–35.
9 Martin, A. J., Papworth, B., Ginns, P. and Malmberg, L. E. (2016), Motivation, engagement, and social climate: An international study of boarding schools, *Journal of Educational Psychology*, 108(6), 772.
10 Bowlby, J. (1969), *Attachment and Loss: Attachment; John Bowlby*. Basic Books, New York.
11 Latham, G. P. and Heslin, P. A. (2003), Training the trainee as well as the trainer: Lessons to be learned from clinical psychology, *Canadian Psychology/Psychologie Canadienne*, 44(3), 218.
12 Carlson, V. J. and Harwood, R. L. (2003), Attachment, culture, and the caregiving system: The cultural patterning of everyday experiences among Anglo and Puerto Rican mother–infant pairs, *Infant Mental Health Journal*, 24(1), 53–73.
13 Chao, R. and Tseng, V. (2002), Parenting of Asians. *Handbook of Parenting*, 4, 59–93.
14 Ullrich-French, S. and Smith, A. L. (2006), Perceptions of relationships with parents and peers in youth sport: Independent and combined prediction of motivational outcomes, *Psychology of Sport and Exercise*, 7(2), 193–214.
15 Maslow, A. H., Frager, R. and Cox, R. (1970), *Motivation and Personality* (Vol. 2, 1,887–1,904), J. Fadiman and C. McReynolds (eds.), Harper & Row, New York.
16 Ybema, S., Keenoy, T., Oswick, C., Beverungen, A. and Ellis, N. (2009), Articulating identities, *Human Relations*, 62(3), 299–322.
17 Berry, J. W. (2005), Acculturation: Living successfully in two cultures, *International Journal of Intercultural Relations*, 29(6), 697–712.
18 Berry, J. W., Phinney, J. S., Sam, D. L. and Vedder, P. (2006), Immigrant youth: Acculturation, identity, and adaptation, *Applied Psychology*, 55(3), 303–332.

19 Duffell, N. (2000), *The Making of Them: The British Attitude to Children and the Boarding School System*, Lone Arrow Press, London, 231.
20 Winnicott, D. W. (1962), *Ego Integration in Child Development: The Maturational Processes and the Facilitating Environment*, New York, International Universities Press.
21 Erikson, E. (1968), *Youth: Identity and Crisis*, W. W. Norton, New York.

FINAL THOUGHTS

Through intelligent, thoughtful and touching narratives, we have shared our childhood stories. We chose to look at the past and the moments each of us holds close in our memory, to bring forward knowledge that can transform our collective awareness of influences of growing up in a boarding school, outside of one's heritage culture. The 'tradition and ethos' of British boarding schools, as stated earlier, is to develop the whole person, to instil self-belief and self-confidence with an emphasis on developing social skills and qualities such as kindness, tolerance and responsibility. So, with such qualities embedded in our identity, we move forward with our lives toward the possibilities that await us. We take comfort in our experience of living in a microcosm of what is today the norm, a diverse and complex environment in which change is consistent. Globalization has changed what was once the prerogative of the rich, forcing mobility among people of all classes of society. As such, our experience of living among the culturally different is no longer limited to the elite.

As children, we were kept in check by mostly absent but authoritarian parents who we believe knew what was best for us. We saw ourselves through their eyes and formulated our identity in an environment where vulnerability impeded us from making decisions about our lives. We learned to comply as well as protect ourselves against change even as we longed for stability and security. As children, we did not have a voice and it would be years before many of us learned to express our feelings and be heard. We were rarely exposed to the opposite sex while at school, so we did not go through the normal trials and tribulations of adolescent girls when it comes to relating to boys except perhaps in our imagination.

In this book, we have taken our readers on a reflective journey to understand and to learn about childhood experiences of foreign children in boarding schools and to witness their resolve as they ventured into the outside world as adults. In retelling fragments of lived experiences of selected Persian women, we have stayed true to the manner, spirit and language in which the story was told; language that is both reflective and at times pragmatic and factual. We travelled with them through their formative adolescent years as they retrospectively scrutinize and deal with the emotional and behavioural dilemmas of growing up while they learned about and adapted to a new culture.

The stories provide a detailed and vivid landscape of everyday life at boarding school, weekend schedule, activities and holiday routine, each with the storyteller's unique perspective and the meanings attributed to it. As such, the stories were often full of emotional and intellectual contradictions. They presented only partial truths, as stories inevitably do. On many occasions, describing emotionally embodied reactions to boarding school experience reproduced joyful or painful moments of our youth. Based on that, there were times when our storytellers chose to make changes, a little tweaking here and there. While reviewing their own stories, some reacted with laughter, 'I can't believe I said that', while others exercised caution by editing phrases saying, 'I don't want to hurt anybody'. The embodied perspective with which each had initially enacted her story gave way to rational processing to take charge once again as it had done in the past. In the end, the stories are ours, an ensemble of how we would like to remember the past, our subjectivity evident in how each of us embraces our heritage and whom we hold accountable for our actions then and now.

We recognized the healing effect of many of these interviews for us. The process of sitting with old and new friends and reminiscing about shared experiences exposed and unlocked many memories of our youth. It brought us closer to each other and perhaps closer to a truer understanding of our own narrative. Through the guided conversations and our collective genuine interest in the topic, many of us claimed to have had a 'purge-like' feeling of our memories. Our reflexivity about the elusive phenomena of boarding school experience shed light on our current lives, while allowing us to visualize the past in a different light. The interviewing process, helped us imagine the future as Catherine Bateson (2010) notes in her book, *Composing a Life*:

> I often have the sense that they are learning from the reawakening of their memories as they retrace the past. Memory is precious, but it is not always clear how to use it or what obligations one has to what has gone before. Looking back over a lifetime takes different forms … There are always surprises, as the remembering and retelling flow into the present and toward the future. Sometimes the answer to 'What next?' is to reach back in time for something that has been neglected, perhaps for years (p. 236).[1]

We found that as our conversations progressed, one memory triggered another and each person's story brought to life a new theme, unfolding a pattern that would then begin to take on a life of its own through the stories of others.

We hold that lives happen in context and, as such, we make no judgment on the nature of the storyteller's subjective experience or the perceived actions of the people in their lives. Underlying our narratives is the understanding that regardless of privilege, adults as parents, live and make choices influenced by the unique circumstances of their own lives. We have a reasonable understanding of our parents' motives for sending us to a foreign land, but we acknowledge that our parents' voice is absent in these narratives. This is in part because we believe that our parents' version of 'truth' today is perhaps as marred as our perceptions, but more importantly because each of us holds a solid position on why we were sent away. The nature of this belief has had a direct impact on how we have each shaped our lives.

As parents, ourselves, we hold our parents to no standard of perfection. We have formulated an understanding and willingness to forgive, and perhaps to make exceptions for them, clearing the past by believing that they 'did their best'. When we were growing up, our parents were involved in their own busy lives and not involved in our day-to-day affairs. As parents ourselves, we have compensated by being perhaps too involved and present in our children's lives. Now, as grandparents, we are witnessing our children's even more increased focus and intense attention to their offspring. We are all doing our best attempting to 'compose a life'.

We note that a key assumption embedded throughout the narrative is our belief that a child has a primary need to be loved, respected and regarded as a person, to be heard and given voice at any given time and in any given environment; that regardless of the experiences of the parents or the nature of the schooling, the notion of respect and tolerance in formative years are critical for the steps towards individuation and autonomy to be taken as an adult. We hold that being loved and valued as a child is at the core of self-esteem and fundamental to the belief in our goodness.

Finally, we draw the attention of our readers to storytelling as a fundamental human activity that not only offers potentially valuable means of eliciting data but also allows for informed criticism of conventional thinking and the development of new paradigms. Our stories were worth telling because of the meanings we personally attached to them. As such, we invite our readers to engage in meaning making of our lives through their own personal stories so that they too may take delight in their own lived experiences.

Note

1   Bateson, C. M., (2010), *Composing a Further Life*, Random House, New York, 236.

APPENDIX I

Our guardian, Mrs Peck

Mr and Mrs John Peck, undated, courtesy of their son, Bahman

Talieh S, affectionately known as Mrs Peck, was an Iranian woman from an upper-class family. She was the guardian to many daughters of Iranian politicians, military officers and businessmen. When we began our research for this book, her son, Bahman, provided us with valuable information about her.

Bahman, who now lives in California, has been a delightful source of information and encouragement, providing us with retrospective memories of his mother from the time he was a young man living in England. Much of the story of Mrs Peck's life is, therefore, told from her son's perspective and for that we are grateful. Bahman also provided helpful vignettes and memories of the girls he remembered who were under the guardianship of Mrs Peck. His comments have not only enriched our stories but have also provided us with an understanding of a woman whose own life was influenced by traditional cultural patterns and attitudes towards women in Iran.

Talieh was born in 1920 in Kashan, a city north of Tehran. She was eight years old when her parents sent her away to Tehran, to live amongst her eight older brothers. It was her brother, Allahyar S, a statesman, who took responsibility for the upbringing of their only sister. An advocate of girls' education, he sent his sister to the American School, Iran Bethal. This was a school established originally as an American missionary organization for women in Tehran, which later became Damavand College, granting undergraduate degrees to women. Talieh completed her education at Tehran University, where she studied English Literature. Listening to Bahman, we wondered whether her choice of schools and guardianship of girls resulted from her own progressive beliefs, shaped in contrast to that of her family's traditional beliefs. She was one of the few women of her generation who attended college in Iran at that time.

At age eighteen, she accepted an arranged marriage to an older man. Talieh was not much older than the children of the man she had just married but, as in other Middle Eastern countries, arranged marriages were the norm in Iran at the time. Couples usually knew of each other through friends and family; sometimes they were even cousins, but the reasons for the marriage varied. Bahman recounts:

> The family wanted my mother to get married and seemed to have accepted the first *khastegar* (suitor). One reason for the haste in getting her to marry my father was the fact that my uncle's household was run by women; his wife, his sister-in-law, and the dominant mother-in-law. They constantly clashed with the young, cheeky Talieh, who knew more about the world than they did, because of her liberal arts education at the Iran Bethal with the American missionaries, her education at University, as well as her inquisitive mind and strong personality. The ladies were therefore rather relieved to get rid of her through marriage!
>
> The marriage was doomed from the start because of the vast difference in their backgrounds. My father was a wealthy older man from Azerbaijan, a historic part of the Persian Empire where people spoke a Turkish dialect and followed a culture somewhat different to the culture my mother was brought

up in. She was a young educated girl from the capital, Tehran. The family had accepted his proposal believing he would be able to take care of her financially.

Bahman was twelve when his parents divorced. He was sent back to his grandmother's home in Kashan, while his mother began pursuing her own dreams. Talieh found a job at the British Embassy and soon became the head of the language school at the British Council in Tehran. This was where she met her second husband, John Peck, a tall, handsome British engineer. Soon after their marriage, Mr and Mrs Peck left Iran for Nigeria, where John was assigned as a telecommunications engineer. In 1957, on the couple's return to England, Mrs Peck travelled back to Iran to accompany her fifteen-year-old son, Bahman, to live with them in London.

Bahman remembers London as a huge contrast to Kashan, where he was brought up with considerable religious and cultural restrictions. After learning English, he continued his education, first in electronics and later in international affairs at London University. During the 1960s and early 1970s, Bahman lived with his mother and stepfather and worked for the Iranian Embassy in London.

He describes his mother as extremely intelligent with a photographic memory; a well-read woman with exceptional knowledge of European history. She was also considered a disciplinarian who instilled fear in her son. We, the authors, shared Bahman's sentiment, remembering Mrs Peck as a tough, strong, no nonsense woman who was the 'absolute boss'.

Ironically, Bahman explains, Mrs Peck's profession as guardian to Persian girls was launched as a favour to Bahman's father, who had asked her to place a friend's children in a boarding school. Though opposed at first, she could not refuse her ex-husband's request:

> At that time, family name was very important. The name was well respected in Iran because the brothers were all educated academics or statesmen. Word got around and the Iranian ambassador, knowing that my mother was acting as a guardian to select Iranian girls, offered her to work with the embassy as advisor to girls who had no form of guardianship when they were sent to England. He believed that her name would carry credibility with prominent Iranian families.

To our knowledge, Mrs Peck was an exception in that she was the only guardian in England at the time who was an Iranian woman.

Bahman recalls that there were many children sent to England to *adam beshand* (become civilized), perhaps without regard for their emotional well-being or the consequences of separation from parents. In some ways, Duffel's *The Making of Them*[1] is a reference to the same notion of *adam beshand* in terms of developing character. But Bahman continues to explain:

> The girls often ended up depressed or committed suicide. In such cases, the schools contacted the Embassy for them to inform the parents. There were

> no cell phones, faxes, or other expedited ways of making contact with Iran other than a long-distance landline telephone service and telegrams, which itself took a few days. My mother was assigned by the Embassy to take care of the most vulnerable girls. At the peak of her career, she was responsible for about forty girls. She terminated her guardianship role toward the end of the 1960s when my parents began a new business venture and returned to Iran. Prior to this time, my mother had partnered with an Armenian woman, Mrs Richards, who took on the responsibility of some of the girls and also rented rooms to students.

When asked about the challenges Mrs Peck faced as a guardian, Bahman recalls a shoplifting incident involving one of the girls that had to be resolved by his mother. He also appreciates the fact that no one got pregnant during his mother's tenure as a guardian! He shared stories about other girls, including a five-year-old who was sent to boarding school because her father remarried and the new wife was not prepared to take care of the little girl. Bahman was a teenager at the time but remembers his mother's concern for the little girl who, he comforts us, later married and was happy! He tells us about his mother's outrage at the affluent and prominent parents who indulged their daughter's extravagant behaviour, such as in one case, asking for and receiving, a fur coat at the age of eighteen.

> My mother never discussed finances with me, but I think she made fifty pounds a year for each student. Since her responsibilities included managing the finances of the children and acting as a liaison for the schools she insisted that parents provide funds for one year of their daughter's expenses in an account available to her for disbursements, such as tuition, holiday travel, visits, clothing, etc.

We asked about Bahman's parents, their relationship with each other and why his mother had chosen to marry an English man.

> Mother needed a husband. She always felt betrayed by her brothers, in particular Dr S—, whom she believed could have facilitated a more favorable marriage with perhaps younger, bachelor doctors whom he knew. So she decided that she had to dig herself out of the situation. She found a good-looking, nice fellow in John and settled. She was always envious of the lives of her cousins who were not as educated or as charming as she, but who had ended up marrying influential politicians. She had, perhaps, a certain amount of resentment towards her own family.

Mrs Peck, the woman who had no relationship with her own mother, and who had experienced very little intimate family life herself, found purpose in her role as a guardian of young girls sent to England. She identified with their sense of separation and abandonment, and became the demi-mother to these girls who were the recipients of her kindness and care, as well as of her admonishment when their behaviour called for it. In her capacity as guardian, she researched the schools, visited the girls to provide guidance and comfort, and made a choice as to which girl to send where. She received the girls' school reports and discussed them with the parents and the girls. We, as her wards, remember Mrs Peck fondly as a charismatic woman, whose stern presence demanded instant respect, reflecting her total confidence and command of the situation. Soosan still remembers Mrs Peck's visits to her school and the occasions when she was taken out for an afternoon tea, her every move observed by the woman who was to become her role model. She has not forgotten the scent of Mrs Peck's Arpege Eau de Parfum and the adolescent dream of becoming *khanoom chic* (chic lady), like Mrs Peck, who always left a trace of her perfume behind as a reminder of her presence!

In their later years, Mr and Mrs Peck made their home in a beautiful ancient village in Spain called Mijas. The majority of the inhabitants there were retired Europeans and the couple loved their lives in this small village. Mrs Peck passed away in 2003 at the age of eighty-three, one year after her husband, John.

Note

1   Duffell, N. (2001), *The Making of Them: The British Attitude to Children and the Boarding School System*, Lone Arrow Press, London, UK.

APPENDIX II

The writing of this book

The purpose of our project was to explore and bring to light the experience of girls in British boarding schools. In particular, we were curious about the cross-cultural experiences of girls, particularly girls from Iran who grew up in British boarding schools.

As coaches, we guide our clients through storytelling, enabling them to discover their world-views based on the meaning they attribute to their lived experiences. Here we chose an interpretive narrative inquiry[1] as a conceptual framework for our project to reveal the socially constructed view of our participants' world. Based on our professional experiences as coaches and educators, we anticipated that interviewing women about their identity, influenced by childhood experiences at a boarding school, would be naturally reflective, possibly contradictory and likely to be emotionally complex. Furthermore, as ex-Persian boarders ourselves, we decided to focus on experiences of Persian girls and adopted both an ethnographic and an auto-ethnographic approach. In doing so, our goal was to account for differences in cultural identity and provide a meaningful expression of our collective social world within the boundaries of Western boarding school experiences.

Qualitative research in general recognizes that there is multiple understanding of what may be considered the 'truth' and that knowledge is embedded in a historical, social and cultural context. In designing our project, based on the Marshall and Rossman (2011)[2] work, we embraced the subjectivity of our participants in sharing their stories. We were also cognizant of our own subjectivity and the possible impact of our interviews on how we interpreted our own childhood. We, therefore, chose to narrate our personal experiences before we began our interviews. We acknowledge that the reflexivity and the subjectivity we brought into the research process by writing our own stories contributed to both the subsequent development of our interview questions as well as our interpretation of other women's stories. Our personal stories provide a detailed and vivid landscape of everyday life at boarding school, each with our own unique perspective. The narrative ability of our participants differed but in retelling their stories, we also aimed to preserve the integrity of each interviewee in terms of her experiences, how she communicated her life story and the manner in which her life was shaped by the 'truth' she held about her childhood.

The stories take our readers on a reflective journey beginning with our questions about the rationale for why we were sent abroad. We attempt to understand who our parents were and the nature of their decision to send their daughters from Iran to England. We look at the absence of our parents and the surrogates we found in other women. In Part II, we reflect on our adolescent years and how we dealt with the emotional and behavioural dilemmas of growing up in a boarding school while we learned about and adapted to a new culture. Part III brings us to our understanding of the women we are today, in light of our childhood experiences, and the subsequent lives we led in Iran and later in the West. We conclude with looking at the lives we shared in Part IV, as we attempt to identify and make meaning of our collective experience and discuss the common themes and patterns that emerge.

This journey began with the most significant curiosity that had brought us together, finding Mrs Peck. We located Mrs Peck's son, Bahman, who currently lives in California. Our goal in speaking to Bahman was to a) learn more about Mrs Peck and b) secure additional names of girls who went to boarding school under her guardianship. Bahman, a delightful source of information and encouragement, provided us with a retrospective on his mother. The story of Mrs Peck's life is thus told from her son's perspective except for when she is remembered within a particular story. His comments provide us with a rich understanding of a woman whose own life was influenced by traditional cultural patterns and attitudes towards women in Iran. Bahman also highlights the fact that there were many other Iranian girls going to boarding school in England at the time, and that not all of them had the privilege of Mrs Peck as their guardian. In response to Bahman's comments, we extended our search for participants to include any Persian girl who went to boarding school during the 1960s and 1970s. We wanted to know whether they too had guardians, and whether they considered the role of a guardian significant in their lives.

Through our social network, we compiled a list of thirty potential participants for our project. We anticipated that most of the women we had identified would have left Iran at some point around the 1979 revolution. We found them in Australia, England, France, Iran, Canada and spread across the U.S. We were unable to connect with many of Mrs Peck's girls and when we did, they did not wish to participate. In the end, ten women agreed to take part in our project (Exhibit I). One (N.) later declined to have her story included in the book.

The stories were revealed to us during face-to-face or Skype interviews, which were facilitated by our guiding questions aimed at evoking adolescent memories (Exhibit II). Baumeister and Newman (1994)[3] state that interpersonal motives and patterns shape the way people tell stories. Whether it is to reward oneself, to have others validate their claims to identity, to simply share information, or to increase one's attraction to others, ultimately stories are shaped by people's need to give meaning to their experiences. These needs include finding purpose, justifying one's own or other's actions, building efficacy and achieving self-worth. Our friendship and interpersonal relations with the interviewees eliminated potential power imbalance between us as well as the need to make a particular impression, but it also presented drawbacks. While our previous knowledge of them provided a strong foundation for sharing of deeply embedded feelings and emotions based on trust, this familiarity also increased our sensitivity and sense of responsibility in how we asked questions, and how we re-told and interpreted their stories. We witnessed our interviewee's struggle and occasional self-monitoring behaviour to stay close to the 'truth' as they recalled and gave meaning to their experiences. We were particularly sensitive to issues of privacy given the very tight social network that we belong to within the Persian community, and chose to eliminate family names using only the first names of the participants.

As a first step, each of us independently analysed each story, as it related to the particular time period our participant had spent at boarding school, and identified recurring themes. The unique anecdotes from each of the women inspired additional questions as we attempted to explore and understand each life story. While compiling the stories, we maintained continuous dialogue with each other through Skype as well as intense working sessions where we identified, (re)interpreted and eventually organized the themes for this book. The stories, as they were told, were then transcribed and sent to the participants for approval. We asked them to delete any information that they may have subsequently decided not to share. We developed a preliminary outline of the book based on the frequency of a theme and its dominance in the story that we were told (Exhibit III). Although there were many similarities, we found that the salient character of each woman made every story unique. A draft of the 'story' was then sent to each participant for her final approval. Several of them made minor corrections and modifications. One participant (we have used initial N to protect her identity) withdrew her story after reading it. She experienced strong emotions reviewing her own story and decided that she did not wish to make it public. She also rejected our offer of anonymity. While her story is not published, the content is reflected in our thematic analysis.

The narratives are both descriptive and reflective, constructed within the context of familiar relationships, to make sense of decades old experiences. They reveal rich and complex perceptions and assumptions that the storytellers hold as partial truth. Resulting from our interpretation, we provide a multidisciplinary social and psychological perspective on girls growing up in a boarding school. We provide our interpretation of the stories throughout the book but highlight significant commonalities in 'Lives we shared', Part IV of the book. We include Mrs Peck's story separately because we were inspired by our discussion of her role as our guardian and wished to both honour her memory but also recognize that her story provides a rich narrative of the traditional life of Persian women who lived a generation before us, perhaps having much in common with our own mothers.

We did not intend to generalize the experiences of these eleven women to all women who have experienced the trauma of boarding school. However, we believe that the particularities of each story are likely to resonate with other ex-boarders and more importantly, with other women in their role as mothers, sisters and daughters. We also hope that by sounding our voice and sharing our stories, we have raised the collective awareness of psychologists and educators on boarding school experience and its impact on young girls' cognitive and emotional development processes.

Notes

1 Chase, S. E. (2005), Narrative Inquiry: Multiple Lenses, Approaches Voices, In Norman K. Denzin and Yvonna S. Lincoln (eds.), *Handbook of Qualitative Research*, Sage Publications, Thousand Oaks, California, 651– 679.
2 Marshall, C. and Rossman, G. B. (2011), *Designing Qualitative Research*, Sage Publications, Thousand Oaks, California.
3 Baumeister, R. F. and Newman, L. S. (1994), How stories make sense of personal experiences: Motives that shape autobiographical narratives, *Personality and Social Psychology Bulletin*, 20(6), 676–690.

EXHIBIT I

The Persian girls' profiles

No	First name	Personal			
		Location	Profession	Education	Age interviewed
1	Soosan*	Toronto	Professor	PhD	61
2	Roya*	Washington	Executive coach	MBA	61
3	Fereshteh	London, UK	Acupunturist	MA	51
4	Saghi	Washington	Home maker	O-levels	51
5	Dory	Washington	Psychologist	MS	51
6	Shirley	London, UK	Philanthropist	BA	61
7	Soheila	Toronto	Accountant	MA	61
8	Shoreh	California	Designer	BA	63
9	Roxane	London, UK	Artist	PhD	60
10	Sheila	California	Pianist	BA	61
11	Azy	California	Businees/ philanthropist	MBA	62
12	N**				

* Peck girls
** Withdrew story

Boarding school				Family		
Year arrived	Age arrived	Age left	School attended	Marital status	Children	Siblings
1965	12	17	Mickelfield	Married(2)	2	3
1964	12	18	Charters Towers	Married	2	2
1974	12	17	Grove School	Divorced	1	2
1973	12	17	Moira House, Chateaubriand	Married	1	3
1976	15	17	Charters Towers, Lowther Collge	Married	1	4
1964	12	17	Charters Towers	Single(2)	2	3
1968	12	16	Mickelfield	Married	2	0
1957	6	17	Godstowe, Hargrove Abbey	Married(2)	0	2
1965	12	18	Charters Towers	Single(1)	2	1
1967	15	18	Mickelfield	Married	0	2
1965	13	18	Charters Towers	Single(1)	2	2

EXHIBIT II

Questions for guided conversation

Boarding school

1. When and where did you go to boarding school (years)?
2. Why did you go?
3. How was it decided for you to go to boarding school?
4. Did anyone from your family go before you?
5. Were there other Persian girls at your school?
6. What was the culture of your school?
7. How did you spend your vacations?
8. Was there a particular teacher that influenced you pedagogically?
9. What kind of influence did that have on you?
10. What were the key events during your years in boarding school?

Guardian/care giver

1. Who was your guardian?
2. What was her role?
3. What influence did that person have on you?
4. How long was she your guardian?
5. What was your relationship with her?
6. What are your memories/experiences of her?
7. Were there others who cared for you?
8. What did you learn from them, if any?

Family

1. What kind of contact did you have with your family? How often?
2. What is your relationship with your siblings?

3. Did you feel loved/unloved by your family?
4. Did you ever feel guilt or need for appreciation of the 'gift' of being sent away?
5. What kind of impact did your parents have on you while you were away? How?
6. What is/was your relationship with your parents during and after your sojourn?
7. What were your parents' expectation of you while at school?
8. What were your parents' expectations when you got back?
9. What were your own expectations for your future life?
10. Did you live your life according to them?

Emotional reactions

1. What was your experience? Positive/negative.
2. How deeply do you feel impacted by your experience?
3. What kind of support system did you have at school?
4. Have you noticed any problems in your adult life as a result of boarding school?
5. Have you noticed any advantages to you as a result of boarding school?
6. Was there ever a feeling of abandonment?
7. What would you describe the challenges you faced at the time?
8. How did you cope in terms of affection, family, love, distance, language, separation, cultural difference?
9. Do you readily show emotion?
10. What strategies for self-protection did you develop that you have kept as a grown up?
11. How do you think those years influenced who you are today (your values, beliefs, how you relate to others, sexuality, culture, arts)?
12. How has your life been shaped as an ex-pat after the revolution?
13. What were your goals, dreams, if any, while at boarding school?
14. What are you doing now?
15. How do you relate what you are doing now to your days in the U.K.?

Role as a woman

1. How would you describe the role of Persian women in 1960s?
2. How has that role changed after the revolution?
3. How would you describe the role of women in the U.K. in 1960s?
4. How has that role changed since?
5. What distinguishes Persian women from women of other societies?
6. What do you see the role of women in today's society?
7. What distinguishes women who had the boarding school experience from other Persian women of their time?
8. How would you have preferred to spend your formative years?
9. What were your dreams as a young girl?
10. Would you be willing to share some pictures of those years and have them in the book?

EXHIBIT III

Classified interview themes

Identity

One way of explaining the girls' experiences might be through the lens of self-concept or identity. Identity is a multi-dimensional construct that may be considered as the culmination of an individual's values, experiences and self-perceptions. Identity development is influenced by challenging environments and experiences that over time result in one's concept of self. How each girl constructs their identity is linked to their childhood experiences and the meaning they attributed to those experiences.

Resilience

A common theme in the stories is the girls' ability to deal with hardships. They were able to bounce back from the trauma of leaving their homes at an early age and resume productive lives. Rather than let this uncontrollable fact overcome them, they ventured into new relationships that ultimately propelled them through their formative years and enabled them to face future adversities. Those with optimistic dispositions were able to leave boarding school years behind with fond memories and an awareness of the impact of the experience on who they were and how they led their lives.

Relationships

What most stories have highlighted is the value of lifelong friendships, ones that have withstood the test of time and distance. The girls pursued different paths in life but the safe environment in which they bonded and the trust they developed in each other continues to shape their relationships today. The stories they shared on a Sunday morning, sitting on the grass outside the dorms, listening to music, waiting for their hair to dry or polishing nails, were different to the stories they are sharing in this book. They learned from each other then, as they are now. Now they are women of different stature, but women who continue to care deeply for each other's wellbeing.

Career versus marriage

The parents' aspirations in sending the girls to the U.K. in pursuit of an elite education seemed to be primarily for them to find a suitable husband and become a 'lady'. At the time, careers were not the priority for the parents or for the girls, whose main objective was to meet the expectations of the parents and, in particular, to marry a suitable man. Many of the girls married at an early age but were divorced soon after. A few remarried while others stayed single. A number of them found a career of their choice and proved themselves capable of independently and successfully managing stressful, demanding, professional lives while maintaining a family.

Leadership

The common adage is 'good leaders are made not born'. Several girls demonstrated their leadership skills from a young age. They refused to conform and actively rebelled against authority, fearless in their behaviour. Others chose to submit to the will of those in charge and in their quiet presence, nurtured their own style of leadership. The impact of their youthful experiences reveals itself in a self-leadership capacity that is not common among many Persian women of their generation.

Trust

The women unequivocally trusted in the authority of their parents. This trust was instrumental in driving their behaviour as young girls. Except for one or two who rebelled in reaction to their predicament, they found themselves 'in check' at the time. Growing up, this trust was extended to teachers and other authority figures. Finding themselves in a new situation, at first they grasped the tails of their guardians who took on the role of the parents. Later at school, siblings and friends were trusted to provide support. In contrast, as adults, the stories and failures of marriages seem to suggest a general lack of trust in other people, an independence and a desire to protect themselves in ways they knew best by keeping their old relationships alive.

Culture/diversity/religion

Born into a homogeneous Iranian culture, while at British boarding schools the girls were exposed to a culture that embraced diversity and celebrated difference. At the time, they were not familiar with or aware of the racism and discrimination that prevailed in other areas of the world. In their innocence, on occasions when racism or discrimination raised its ugly head, they were able to quickly dispel and move forward with harmony. This understanding of differences has served them well living in the West after the Iranian Revolution. They were not religious but turned to faith at times of despair to express pent up emotions.

Discipline

In Iran, the girls were expected to conduct themselves according to the norms of the Iranian society with little personal responsibility for their own day-to-day welfare. This changed when they began living in England. The British culture, as well as the rules and regulations of the boarding school's heavily structured daily schedule, forced them to follow a strict discipline. In addition, they were given responsibility for managing much of their own lives outside of school. They did so with just as much discipline and maturity. They acquired a set of values and discipline at an early age that seems to have continued to influence their behaviour as adults.

Integrity/honesty

The standards of integrity and honesty that were instilled in them at school reinforced the values they were exposed to through their upbringing in their families. For the most part they remain loyal to their friends and family members believing in doing good to protect their honour. To them, character is all that matters.

Abandonment and denial/guilt

The sense of abandonment was experienced by many of the girls when they were left behind, feeling deprived of the love of parents in their formative years. Their response to these sentiments is influenced as much by their individual personality as the family and school environment in which they grew up. In their attempt to preserve the self, they relied on the inevitable forces of denial and guilt to meet the expectations of parents, who they were led to believe provided them with the opportunity for a better life. Whether they chose conformity or rebellion, optimism or cynicism, the deeply embedded feelings have significantly impacted how they relate to authority as well as how they form and maintain productive relationships with others.

Loneliness

Despite the support group that many of the girls had developed around themselves, the pangs of loneliness and yearning were omnipresent throughout the stories. Each girl demonstrated and handled these sentiments differently, many through letter writing practices to ensure they were not forgotten, listening to music that carried them to happier places or weekly get togethers with other girls to reminisce about their families and homes.

The educators

Many of the educators were single women or widows of the Second World War. Their husbands or boyfriends had been taken away from them at a young age to serve and never returned. They had a rather callous attitude toward young girls, who far from their loved ones, needed love and attention. Their nervous twitches amused the girls, while their strict demeanour and strong presence triggered fear and anxiety.

INDEX

Abadan 78, 79, 84n1
acculturation process 133; orientation style 134
adolescence 46
Afrooz, Novin 80, 84n3
Alam (Dr), Imran 88
A-Levels 22n3, 53
Angelou, Maya 45, 127
attention deficit hyperactivity disorder (ADHD) 38
Azy 130, 135; Heidi (sister) 132; Iranian Scholarship Foundation 137; profile 154
Azy, boarding experience: attention deficit and business 38; away from revolution 33; changing lifestyle 35; coping up 33–4; gaining ability 37; homosexuality 32; Iranian versus Western girls 32; Roxane 32; Roya 32, 34, 36; self-esteem 38; self-made armour 33; Shirley 32, 34, 36
Azy's family: grandfather's love 35–6; Iranian Scholarship Fund 39; philanthropist 39; spirituality and religious beliefs 36; uncaring parents 35; younger sister 36–7
Azy's teachers/guardians: McGarry (Miss), the headmistress 32, 34; Thomson (Mrs) 35, 41

Baldner, Thomas 80
Bass, L. R. 127
Baumeister, R. F. 151
belief in goodness 143
Berry, J. W. 134
bicultural identity 134, 137

boarding experience *see individual boarding experience*
boarding schools: need for 87; traumatic experience 99
boarding school syndrome 128
Bodelwyddan Castle 62, 66n3
Bowlby, J. 129
British boarding school xi; adolescent years 151; childhood experiences and subsequent lives 151; cognitive and emotional development processes 153; collective experience 151; experience of girls in 150; Iran to England 151; tradition and ethos 141; *see also individual schools*
The British Journal of Psychiatry 128
British social etiquette 122
Brown, L. M. 129

Camelot's Kitchen (Shoreh) 125
Carlson, V. J. 130
Carmel College, Newbury 68, 75n1
Caspian Sea 24, 30n1, 108
casualties 128
chador 61, 66n1
Chao, R. 130
Charters Towers School, Sussex: Azy in 31; Dory in 60, 61; Roxane in 85; Roya in 7, 9, 12; Shirley in 67, 68
Chateaubriand School, France 58; Saghi in 49
child abuse 10, 66n4, 128; mental abuse 66n4; physical abuse 63, 66n4
civilization 136
compliers 128

Composing a Life (Bateson) 142
consumers, women as 3
cross-cultural layer xi
crush 15, 18, 46, 71, 91
cultural dichotomy 129
cultural values 135
culture of character 136
culture of personality 136

Damavand College (formerly Iran Bethal) 109, 110n2, 146
David and Goliath (Gladwell) 92
Delbar (Iranian girl) 80
doing and being 100
Dory 132, 134; communication 95; hatred towards parents 130; irretrievable detachment 96; Marjaneh (sister) 62, 66; nonreligious family 61; Omid Foundation 138; profile 154
Dory, boarding experience 61; aptitude for reading people 64; autograph books 65; father's decision 61; Foster (Mr), teacher 62; homosexual behaviour 62; introvert 64; pregnant girls 65; self-improvement 65; submissive nature 63; survival method 63; trauma treatment 63
Duffell, N. 128

early boarding 131
Eaton (Mrs) 132, 133
Elias, B. 127
emotions 99
Englishness 133
English system, trust in 28
Erikson 135
Etefagh School, Tehran 68, 75n2
exeats 16, 22n2; Diana (friend) and Roya 16–17; Roxane 86, 88, 89; Roya 16, 17; Shirley 17, 69, 71
experience abroad *see individual boarding experience*

family expectations 135
Farsi versus English 135
The Feminine Mystique (Friedan) 3
Fereshteh: cosmic elements 137; profile 154
Fereshteh, boarding experience: awkward situations 26–7; daddy-long-legs 25; dream to become interpreter 28; eating habit 26; English culture 28; German summer school 27; item list 24–5; jail like feeling 25; learning English 27; mixed experience 27; reconciliation 29; rhododendron walk 26; self-reliant 28; single failure 24; Summer school 24

Frank, Anne 108
French 133
Freudian therapy 89

Gandhi's words 139
Gilligan, Carol 46, 129
Ginns, P. 127
globalization 141
Godstowe School, Buckinghamshire: Shoreh in 111
The Grove School, Surrey: Fereshteh in 23, 24, 27, 28
guardian, role of 87

Hadaf High School 121, 124n1
Hafez (Iranian poet) 83, 84n4
Hargrove Abbey, Buckinghamshire: Shoreh in 111
harshness 19
Harvard, feminist environment 92
Harwood, R. L. 130
healing effect 142
Heslin, P. A. 129
Hogwarts School of Witchcraft and Wizardry 62, 66n2
homosexuality 15, 32, 62

independent thinkers 46
interpretive narrative inquiry 150
interview themes: abandonment 159; career versus marriage 158; culture 158–9; denial 159; discipline 159; diversity 158–9; educators 160; guilt 159; honesty 159; identity 157; integrity 159; leadership 158; loneliness 159; relationships 157–8; religion 158–9; resilience 157; trust 158
Iran: birth of boy baby 4; education abroad 5; education of women 4; family culture 3; legal system 4; maternal love 5; paternal discipline 5; sexual interactions 5; upper-class family values 5
Iranian Revolution of 1979 xii
Iranians: biases 137; parents' decision 47; privileged-class families 45; stay-at-home moms 45
Iranian women xi
Iran/Iraq war 29, 30n2

joon (life) 57, 59n4

Keller, Helen 99
Khomeini, Ayatollah Ruhollah xii
Kids Go Classical program 83
Kipling, Rudyard 53

Latham, G. P. 129
Liem, G. A. D. 127
Lives we shared 152
Lowther College, North Wales: Dory in 60, 61, 62, 63

Magic of Persia Foundation 75
The Making of Them (Duffel) 147
The Making of Them (film) 100, 100n2
mandatory maturity 41
Marshall, C. 150
Martin, A. J. 127
Maslow, A. H. 133
McDowell, L. 46
McGarry (Miss) 132
Micklefield School, Sussex 136, 137; Shelia in 76, 78; Soheila 120; Soosan in 101, 104
Millfield School 88
misogyny xii
Moira House, Sussex 49, 52, 57, 58
Molana (Persian poet) 83

Namaz, Muslim prayer 15, 22n1, 61
National Iranian Oil Company (NIOC) executives 77
Newman, L. S. 151
Nicholas Nickleby (la Dickens) 128
1979 Islamic Revolution xii, 45, 84n1
non-English privileged families 127
Nowruz (new day), 104, 110n1

O-Levels 21, 22n3, 53
Omid Foundation 66, 66n4
only child syndrome 90

Pahlavi Dynasty xii
Pahlavi, Mohammad Reza Shah xii, 3, 4
Papworth, B. 127
parenting, change in 29
parenting style 129; freedom from 135; socio-emotional wellbeing 130
parents' decision 40, 41
Peck (Mrs) 132–3, 145, 146, 151; *adam beshand* (become civilized) 147; Bahman (son) 146, 151; challenges 148; charismatic 149; divorce 147; English man, marriage 148; husband 146; Mijas 149; Saleh, Allahyar (brother) 146
Persian girls xii; coping xiii
Persian *taarof* 56, 59n3
Peykan Javanan 50, 58n1
positive parenting 129
power 46

pre-revolution *taghootis* 75, 75n4
professional reputation 40
psychological attachment theory 129
'purge-like' feeling 142

qualitative research 150
questions for guided conversation: boarding school 155; emotional reactions 156; family 155–6; guardian/care giver 155; role as woman 156
Quran 50; passing under the Quran 59n2

rebels 128
residential educational program 127
restrictive communitarianism 134
Richard, Cliff (singer) 108
Rossman, G. B. 150
Roxane 130, 131; Middle Eastern Art director 138; profile 154; resilience 96; sense of assurance 96
Roxane, boarding experience 85; anxious by nature 90; bathing 90–1; career minded 92; closeness with father 93; divorce 94; Eaton (Mrs) 86, 87; English versus Farsi 86; *exeat* 86; hair washing 91; independent nature 94; learned behaviour 93; Manfred (Miss), headmistress 86; McGarry (Miss), 91; missing social skills 90; only child syndrome 90; residential nursery 86; self-esteem issues 93; self-sufficient person 92; separation anxiety 89; sleeping with open windows 90; Smith (Miss), Palmer 86; support from friends 91
Roya 7; air travel 9; 'Americanized' atmosphere 9; balanced life 138; close enduring friendships 130; international communication 9–10; profile 154; summer camp 8; teacher/parent conference 8; traditional role 136; travel to school 8; Vida (sister) 11, 12, 132
Roya, boarding experience: Christmas, British traditions 19; crush 15; dating 21; discipline, from father 21; entertainment 14, 15; *exeats* 16–17; holiday home 19; homosexuality 15; mealtime fun 14; midnight feast 17–18; mother's visit 17, 20; roommate 13; schedule of errands 12; school, looks of 13; skiing 20; star's visit 17; Sundays 15–16; Switzerland trip 19–20
Roya, experience abroad 10; emotional difficulties 11; excitement 11; Vida (sister), support 11, 12

Roya's teachers/guides: Butterfield (Mrs) 18; Elliott (Miss) 18; Foster (Mr) 18; McGarry (Miss), headmistress 14, 15, 17, 19; Peck (Mrs) 11, 12, 13, 21; piano teacher 19; Sharpus (Miss) 13; Wray (Mrs) 18

Rumi *see* Molana (Persian poet)

Saghi 49, 50, 132, 133, 134, 138; costume parties 55; cultural upbringing 56; culture shock 95; naughtiness 56; profile 154; and Roya 50; Saghi to Sally 95

Saghi, boarding experience: becoming independent 56; better education 50; British characteristics 52; English speaking 52; father's support 57; fear 52; France experience 58; hermaphrodite 52–3; kitchen work 55; parents' decision 52; Prince Salim 54; racism 53; Saghi to Sally 51; Sally to Saghi 58; trip in ferry 50

Saghi's teachers/guides: Hyde (Mrs) 51; Underwood (Mr) 55

Saleh, Talieh *see* Peck (Mrs)

Schaverien, J. 127, 128, 131

self-belief 128, 141

self-confidence 128, 136, 141

self-control 46

self-esteem 38, 56, 93, 143

self-monitoring behaviour 152

self-respect 46

self-worth 152

sex objects, women as 3

sexual harassment 29

sexual revolution 3

Sharpus, Matron 68

Sheila 76; brother's health 80–1; guitar practice 79; likeminded people 81; marriage 82; music 131; Nikolsky, Aleksey (husband) 81, 82, 83; Persian classical music 138; Persian music(ian) 82, 96; preparing to England trip 78; profile 154; refuge at piano 96; science fiction books 79; solo piano pieces 77; Soosan and 77; University of Southern California (USC) 81; Western music 82

Sheila, boarding experience: design drawings 80; leadership position 80; piano practice 79; Soosan and 79; Woods (Mrs), headmistress 78

Shirley 67, 130, 135; bigotry 96; boyfriend 72; *exeats* 69; exposure to art 72–3; Flora (sister) 132; Magic of Persia 138; Mahnaz (cousin), wedding 72; marriage 72, 73; profile 154; rebellious performance 96; self-confidence 136

Shirley, boarding experience: and Azy 71; holidays 72; interrogation 70; ladder girl 70; letter-writing period 71; managing anger 74; McGarry (Miss) 69; money and status 73–4; multi-racial culture 70; naughty tricks 70, 71; network of people 74; older sister as guardian 68, 69; roommate 68–9; Roya 69; self-made religious period 71; team spirit and competitiveness 73; travel 68

Shoreh 138; *Camelot's Kitchen* 125; creative artist 118; Farsi versus English 118; feeling of homelessness 125, 130; Fox (Mrs), guardian 132; Guilda (sister) 132; homeless feeling 117–18; married life 119; profile 154; self-sufficient person 119

Shoreh, boarding experience 111; A-Levels 116, 117; best friends 115; *Camelot's Kitchen* 113; Farhad (cousin) 113; Ferrier (Madame), French teacher 115; Fisher (Ms), headmistress 114; Fox (Mrs) 112; Guilda (sister) 112, 113–14; hardest walk 116; love 115; McNab (Miss), German teacher 115; and Roya 112; sexual revolution 115; Ziba (friend) 117

Skype interview 151, 152

Soheila 120, 130, 131, 137; Association of Professional Language Interpreters 124, 138; chartered accountant 124; commitment to Persian culture 126; defending refugees in Canadian courts of law 126; profile 154; and Soosan 121; trip to London 121

Soheila, boarding experience: academically focused 124; British social etiquette 122; courage 123–4; Cynthia (assigned mentor) 123; English proficiency 122; mixed feeling 122; Shokouh Joon (mother) 122

Soosan 101; civil rights movement 108; Martha (friend) 108; miniskirt fashion 108; parents' belief in Western values 107; profile 154; secure contented life 125; *sheitoon* (mischievous or naughty) 105; Sudi (sister) 102, 132; York University professor 138

Soosan, boarding experience: amazing experience 106; Barbara (English friend) 108; courteous words 104; Delbar (friend) 104; exhilarated feeling 102; feeling liberated 102; international friends 106; introvert 106; Iranian

friends 106; Nicklen family, holidays 108; O-Levels 105; Peck (Mrs), guardian 102, 103; Peyton (Mrs), teacher 105; school uniform 103; self-care 107; separation 109; trip to London 102
Spencer, S. 46
Strategic Survival Personality 128
supportive behaviours 131
Synergo Music Method 83

Thomson (Mrs) 132
Tirimo, Martino 84n2; Royal Academy of Music 80
To Love and Serve 136, 137
'Top of the Pops', television show 14, 53, 105
Tseng, V. 130

University of Cambridge 66, 114, 117
University of Southern California (USC) 81
University of Tehran 11, 21

Western culture 136
Western individualism 134
White Revolution 3, 6n2
women upkeep 10
www.boardingrecovery.com 128
www.boardingschoolsurvivors.co.uk 128

Ybema, H. 133

young professionals 10

Zan-e-Rooz (women magazine) 72, 75n3